C-4769 CAREER EXAMINATION SERIES

This is your PASSBOOK for...

Code Enforcement Inspector Trainee

Test Preparation Study Guide
Questions & Answers

NLC®

NATIONAL LEARNING CORPORATION®

National Learning Corporation

212 Michael Drive, Syosset, NY 11791
(516) 921-8888 • www.passbooks.com
E-mail: info@passbooks.com

PASSBOOK® SERIES

THE *PASSBOOK® SERIES* has been created to prepare applicants and candidates for the ultimate academic battlefield – the examination room.

At some time in our lives, each and every one of us may be required to take an examination – for validation, matriculation, admission, qualification, registration, certification, or licensure.

Based on the assumption that every applicant or candidate has met the basic formal educational standards, has taken the required number of courses, and read the necessary texts, the *PASSBOOK® SERIES* furnishes the one special preparation which may assure passing with confidence, instead of failing with insecurity. Examination questions – together with answers – are furnished as the basic vehicle for study so that the mysteries of the examination and its compounding difficulties may be eliminated or diminished by a sure method.

This book is meant to help you pass your examination provided that you qualify and are serious in your objective.

The entire field is reviewed through the huge store of content information which is succinctly presented through a provocative and challenging approach – the question-and-answer method.

A climate of success is established by furnishing the correct answers at the end of each test.

You soon learn to recognize types of questions, forms of questions, and patterns of questioning. You may even begin to anticipate expected outcomes.

You perceive that many questions are repeated or adapted so that you can gain acute insights, which may enable you to score many sure points.

You learn how to confront new questions, or types of questions, and to attack them confidently and work out the correct answers.

You note objectives and emphases, and recognize pitfalls and dangers, so that you may make positive educational adjustments.

Moreover, you are kept fully informed in relation to new concepts, methods, practices, and directions in the field.

You discover that you are actually taking the examination all the time: you are preparing for the examination by "taking" an examination, not by reading extraneous and/or supererogatory textbooks.

In short, this PASSBOOK®, used directedly, should be an important factor in helping you to pass your test.

CODE ENFORCEMENT INSPECTOR TRAINEE

DUTIES:

Under direct supervision, assists Code Enforcement Inspectors, and receives training in performing inspections to enforce various village ordinances and codes such as, zoning, housing and rehabilitation, refuse, streets and sidewalks, fire prevention and control, and other similar ones; performs related duties as required.

SUBJECT OF EXAMINATION:

The written test is designed to test for knowledge, skills, and/or abilities in the following areas:

1. **Evaluating information and evidence** - These questions test for the ability to evaluate and draw conclusions from information and evidence. Each question consists of a set of facts and a conclusion based on the facts. The candidate must decide if the conclusion is warranted by the facts.
2. **Preparing written material** - These questions test for the ability to present information clearly and accurately, and to organize paragraphs logically and comprehensibly. For some questions, you will be given information in two or three sentences followed by four restatements of the information. You must then choose the best version. For other questions, you will be given paragraphs with their sentences out of order. You must then choose, from four suggestions, the best order for the sentences.
3. **Understanding and interpreting written material** - These questions test for the ability to understand and interpret written material. You will be presented with brief reading passages and will be asked questions about the passages.

HOW TO TAKE A TEST

I. YOU MUST PASS AN EXAMINATION

A. WHAT EVERY CANDIDATE SHOULD KNOW

Examination applicants often ask us for help in preparing for the written test. What can I study in advance? What kinds of questions will be asked? How will the test be given? How will the papers be graded?

As an applicant for a civil service examination, you may be wondering about some of these things. Our purpose here is to suggest effective methods of advance study and to describe civil service examinations.

Your chances for success on this examination can be increased if you know how to prepare. Those "pre-examination jitters" can be reduced if you know what to expect. You can even experience an adventure in good citizenship if you know why civil service exams are given.

B. WHY ARE CIVIL SERVICE EXAMINATIONS GIVEN?

Civil service examinations are important to you in two ways. As a citizen, you want public jobs filled by employees who know how to do their work. As a job seeker, you want a fair chance to compete for that job on an equal footing with other candidates. The best-known means of accomplishing this two-fold goal is the competitive examination.

Exams are widely publicized throughout the nation. They may be administered for jobs in federal, state, city, municipal, town or village governments or agencies.

Any citizen may apply, with some limitations, such as the age or residence of applicants. Your experience and education may be reviewed to see whether you meet the requirements for the particular examination. When these requirements exist, they are reasonable and applied consistently to all applicants. Thus, a competitive examination may cause you some uneasiness now, but it is your privilege and safeguard.

C. HOW ARE CIVIL SERVICE EXAMS DEVELOPED?

Examinations are carefully written by trained technicians who are specialists in the field known as "psychological measurement," in consultation with recognized authorities in the field of work that the test will cover. These experts recommend the subject matter areas or skills to be tested; only those knowledges or skills important to your success on the job are included. The most reliable books and source materials available are used as references. Together, the experts and technicians judge the difficulty level of the questions.

Test technicians know how to phrase questions so that the problem is clearly stated. Their ethics do not permit "trick" or "catch" questions. Questions may have been tried out on sample groups, or subjected to statistical analysis, to determine their usefulness.

Written tests are often used in combination with performance tests, ratings of training and experience, and oral interviews. All of these measures combine to form the best-known means of finding the right person for the right job.

II. HOW TO PASS THE WRITTEN TEST

A. NATURE OF THE EXAMINATION

To prepare intelligently for civil service examinations, you should know how they differ from school examinations you have taken. In school you were assigned certain definite pages to read or subjects to cover. The examination questions were quite detailed and usually emphasized memory. Civil service exams, on the other hand, try to discover your present ability to perform the duties of a position, plus your potentiality to learn these duties. In other words, a civil service exam attempts to predict how successful you will be. Questions cover such a broad area that they cannot be as minute and detailed as school exam questions.

In the public service similar kinds of work, or positions, are grouped together in one "class." This process is known as *position-classification.* All the positions in a class are paid according to the salary range for that class. One class title covers all of these positions, and they are all tested by the same examination.

B. FOUR BASIC STEPS

1) Study the announcement

How, then, can you know what subjects to study? Our best answer is: "Learn as much as possible about the class of positions for which you've applied." The exam will test the knowledge, skills and abilities needed to do the work.

Your most valuable source of information about the position you want is the official exam announcement. This announcement lists the training and experience qualifications. Check these standards and apply only if you come reasonably close to meeting them.

The brief description of the position in the examination announcement offers some clues to the subjects which will be tested. Think about the job itself. Review the duties in your mind. Can you perform them, or are there some in which you are rusty? Fill in the blank spots in your preparation.

Many jurisdictions preview the written test in the exam announcement by including a section called "Knowledge and Abilities Required," "Scope of the Examination," or some similar heading. Here you will find out specifically what fields will be tested.

2) Review your own background

Once you learn in general what the position is all about, and what you need to know to do the work, ask yourself which subjects you already know fairly well and which need improvement. You may wonder whether to concentrate on improving your strong areas or on building some background in your fields of weakness. When the announcement has specified "some knowledge" or "considerable knowledge," or has used adjectives like "beginning principles of..." or "advanced ... methods," you can get a clue as to the number and difficulty of questions to be asked in any given field. More questions, and hence broader coverage, would be included for those subjects which are more important in the work. Now weigh your strengths and weaknesses against the job requirements and prepare accordingly.

3) Determine the level of the position

Another way to tell how intensively you should prepare is to understand the level of the job for which you are applying. Is it the entering level? In other words, is this the position in which beginners in a field of work are hired? Or is it an intermediate or advanced level? Sometimes this is indicated by such words as "Junior" or "Senior" in the class title. Other jurisdictions use Roman numerals to designate the level – Clerk I, Clerk II, for example. The word "Supervisor" sometimes appears in the title. If the level is not indicated by the title, check the description of duties. Will you be working under very close supervision, or will you have responsibility for independent decisions in this work?

4) Choose appropriate study materials

Now that you know the subjects to be examined and the relative amount of each subject to be covered, you can choose suitable study materials. For beginning level jobs, or even advanced ones, if you have a pronounced weakness in some aspect of your training, read a modern, standard textbook in that field. Be sure it is up to date and has general coverage. Such books are normally available at your library, and the librarian will be glad to help you locate one. For entry-level positions, questions of appropriate difficulty are chosen – neither highly advanced questions, nor those too simple. Such questions require careful thought but not advanced training.

If the position for which you are applying is technical or advanced, you will read more advanced, specialized material. If you are already familiar with the basic principles of your field, elementary textbooks would waste your time. Concentrate on advanced textbooks and technical periodicals. Think through the concepts and review difficult problems in your field.

These are all general sources. You can get more ideas on your own initiative, following these leads. For example, training manuals and publications of the government agency which employs workers in your field can be useful, particularly for technical and professional positions. A letter or visit to the government department involved may result in more specific study suggestions, and certainly will provide you with a more definite idea of the exact nature of the position you are seeking.

III. KINDS OF TESTS

Tests are used for purposes other than measuring knowledge and ability to perform specified duties. For some positions, it is equally important to test ability to make adjustments to new situations or to profit from training. In others, basic mental abilities not dependent on information are essential. Questions which test these things may not appear as pertinent to the duties of the position as those which test for knowledge and information. Yet they are often highly important parts of a fair examination. For very general questions, it is almost impossible to help you direct your study efforts. What we can do is to point out some of the more common of these general abilities needed in public service positions and describe some typical questions.

1) General information

Broad, general information has been found useful for predicting job success in some kinds of work. This is tested in a variety of ways, from vocabulary lists to questions about current events. Basic background in some field of work, such as sociology or economics, may be sampled in a group of questions. Often these are principles which have become familiar to most persons through exposure rather than through formal training. It is difficult to advise you how to study for these questions; being alert to the world around you is our best suggestion.

2) Verbal ability

An example of an ability needed in many positions is verbal or language ability. Verbal ability is, in brief, the ability to use and understand words. Vocabulary and grammar tests are typical measures of this ability. Reading comprehension or paragraph interpretation questions are common in many kinds of civil service tests. You are given a paragraph of written material and asked to find its central meaning.

3) Numerical ability

Number skills can be tested by the familiar arithmetic problem, by checking paired lists of numbers to see which are alike and which are different, or by interpreting charts and graphs. In the latter test, a graph may be printed in the test booklet which you are asked to use as the basis for answering questions.

4) Observation

A popular test for law-enforcement positions is the observation test. A picture is shown to you for several minutes, then taken away. Questions about the picture test your ability to observe both details and larger elements.

5) Following directions

In many positions in the public service, the employee must be able to carry out written instructions dependably and accurately. You may be given a chart with several columns, each column listing a variety of information. The questions require you to carry out directions involving the information given in the chart.

6) Skills and aptitudes

Performance tests effectively measure some manual skills and aptitudes. When the skill is one in which you are trained, such as typing or shorthand, you can practice. These tests are often very much like those given in business school or high school courses. For many of the other skills and aptitudes, however, no short-time preparation can be made. Skills and abilities natural to you or that you have developed throughout your lifetime are being tested.

Many of the general questions just described provide all the data needed to answer the questions and ask you to use your reasoning ability to find the answers. Your best preparation for these tests, as well as for tests of facts and ideas, is to be at your physical and mental best. You, no doubt, have your own methods of getting into an exam-taking mood and keeping "in shape." The next section lists some ideas on this subject.

IV. KINDS OF QUESTIONS

Only rarely is the "essay" question, which you answer in narrative form, used in civil service tests. Civil service tests are usually of the short-answer type. Full instructions for answering these questions will be given to you at the examination. But in case this is your first experience with short-answer questions and separate answer sheets, here is what you need to know:

1) Multiple-choice Questions

Most popular of the short-answer questions is the "multiple choice" or "best answer" question. It can be used, for example, to test for factual knowledge, ability to solve problems or judgment in meeting situations found at work.

A multiple-choice question is normally one of three types—

- It can begin with an incomplete statement followed by several possible endings. You are to find the one ending which *best* completes the statement, although some of the others may not be entirely wrong.
- It can also be a complete statement in the form of a question which is answered by choosing one of the statements listed.

- It can be in the form of a problem – again you select the best answer.

Here is an example of a multiple-choice question with a discussion which should give you some clues as to the method for choosing the right answer:

When an employee has a complaint about his assignment, the action which will *best* help him overcome his difficulty is to
A. discuss his difficulty with his coworkers
B. take the problem to the head of the organization
C. take the problem to the person who gave him the assignment
D. say nothing to anyone about his complaint

In answering this question, you should study each of the choices to find which is best. Consider choice "A" – Certainly an employee may discuss his complaint with fellow employees, but no change or improvement can result, and the complaint remains unresolved. Choice "B" is a poor choice since the head of the organization probably does not know what assignment you have been given, and taking your problem to him is known as "going over the head" of the supervisor. The supervisor, or person who made the assignment, is the person who can clarify it or correct any injustice. Choice "C" is, therefore, correct. To say nothing, as in choice "D," is unwise. Supervisors have and interest in knowing the problems employees are facing, and the employee is seeking a solution to his problem.

2) True/False Questions

The "true/false" or "right/wrong" form of question is sometimes used. Here a complete statement is given. Your job is to decide whether the statement is right or wrong.

SAMPLE: A roaming cell-phone call to a nearby city costs less than a non-roaming call to a distant city.

This statement is wrong, or false, since roaming calls are more expensive.

This is not a complete list of all possible question forms, although most of the others are variations of these common types. You will always get complete directions for answering questions. Be sure you understand *how* to mark your answers – ask questions until you do.

V. RECORDING YOUR ANSWERS

Computer terminals are used more and more today for many different kinds of exams.

For an examination with very few applicants, you may be told to record your answers in the test booklet itself. Separate answer sheets are much more common. If this separate answer sheet is to be scored by machine – and this is often the case – it is highly important that you mark your answers correctly in order to get credit.

An electronic scoring machine is often used in civil service offices because of the speed with which papers can be scored. Machine-scored answer sheets must be marked with a pencil, which will be given to you. This pencil has a high graphite content which responds to the electronic scoring machine. As a matter of fact, stray dots may register as answers, so do not let your pencil rest on the answer sheet while you are pondering the correct answer. Also, if your pencil lead breaks or is otherwise defective, ask for another.

Since the answer sheet will be dropped in a slot in the scoring machine, be careful not to bend the corners or get the paper crumpled.

The answer sheet normally has five vertical columns of numbers, with 30 numbers to a column. These numbers correspond to the question numbers in your test booklet. After each number, going across the page are four or five pairs of dotted lines. These short dotted lines have small letters or numbers above them. The first two pairs may also have a "T" or "F" above the letters. This indicates that the first two pairs only are to be used if the questions are of the true-false type. If the questions are multiple choice, disregard the "T" and "F" and pay attention only to the small letters or numbers.

Answer your questions in the manner of the sample that follows:

32. The largest city in the United States is
    - A. Washington, D.C.
    - B. New York City
    - C. Chicago
    - D. Detroit
    - E. San Francisco

1) Choose the answer you think is best. (New York City is the largest, so "B" is correct.)
2) Find the row of dotted lines numbered the same as the question you are answering. (Find row number 32)
3) Find the pair of dotted lines corresponding to the answer. (Find the pair of lines under the mark "B.")
4) Make a solid black mark between the dotted lines.

VI. BEFORE THE TEST

Common sense will help you find procedures to follow to get ready for an examination. Too many of us, however, overlook these sensible measures. Indeed, nervousness and fatigue have been found to be the most serious reasons why applicants fail to do their best on civil service tests. Here is a list of reminders:

- Begin your preparation early – Don't wait until the last minute to go scurrying around for books and materials or to find out what the position is all about.
- Prepare continuously – An hour a night for a week is better than an all-night cram session. This has been definitely established. What is more, a night a week for a month will return better dividends than crowding your study into a shorter period of time.
- Locate the place of the exam – You have been sent a notice telling you when and where to report for the examination. If the location is in a different town or otherwise unfamiliar to you, it would be well to inquire the best route and learn something about the building.
- Relax the night before the test – Allow your mind to rest. Do not study at all that night. Plan some mild recreation or diversion; then go to bed early and get a good night's sleep.
- Get up early enough to make a leisurely trip to the place for the test – This way unforeseen events, traffic snarls, unfamiliar buildings, etc. will not upset you.
- Dress comfortably – A written test is not a fashion show. You will be known by number and not by name, so wear something comfortable.

- Leave excess paraphernalia at home – Shopping bags and odd bundles will get in your way. You need bring only the items mentioned in the official notice you received; usually everything you need is provided. Do not bring reference books to the exam. They will only confuse those last minutes and be taken away from you when in the test room.
- Arrive somewhat ahead of time – If because of transportation schedules you must get there very early, bring a newspaper or magazine to take your mind off yourself while waiting.
- Locate the examination room – When you have found the proper room, you will be directed to the seat or part of the room where you will sit. Sometimes you are given a sheet of instructions to read while you are waiting. Do not fill out any forms until you are told to do so; just read them and be prepared.
- Relax and prepare to listen to the instructions
- If you have any physical problem that may keep you from doing your best, be sure to tell the test administrator. If you are sick or in poor health, you really cannot do your best on the exam. You can come back and take the test some other time.

VII. AT THE TEST

The day of the test is here and you have the test booklet in your hand. The temptation to get going is very strong. Caution! There is more to success than knowing the right answers. You must know how to identify your papers and understand variations in the type of short-answer question used in this particular examination. Follow these suggestions for maximum results from your efforts:

1) Cooperate with the monitor

The test administrator has a duty to create a situation in which you can be as much at ease as possible. He will give instructions, tell you when to begin, check to see that you are marking your answer sheet correctly, and so on. He is not there to guard you, although he will see that your competitors do not take unfair advantage. He wants to help you do your best.

2) Listen to all instructions

Don't jump the gun! Wait until you understand all directions. In most civil service tests you get more time than you need to answer the questions. So don't be in a hurry. Read each word of instructions until you clearly understand the meaning. Study the examples, listen to all announcements and follow directions. Ask questions if you do not understand what to do.

3) Identify your papers

Civil service exams are usually identified by number only. You will be assigned a number; you must not put your name on your test papers. Be sure to copy your number correctly. Since more than one exam may be given, copy your exact examination title.

4) Plan your time

Unless you are told that a test is a "speed" or "rate of work" test, speed itself is usually not important. Time enough to answer all the questions will be provided, but this does not mean that you have all day. An overall time limit has been set. Divide the total time (in minutes) by the number of questions to determine the approximate time you have for each question.

5) Do not linger over difficult questions

If you come across a difficult question, mark it with a paper clip (useful to have along) and come back to it when you have been through the booklet. One caution if you do this – be sure to skip a number on your answer sheet as well. Check often to be sure that you have not lost your place and that you are marking in the row numbered the same as the question you are answering.

6) Read the questions

Be sure you know what the question asks! Many capable people are unsuccessful because they failed to *read* the questions correctly.

7) Answer all questions

Unless you have been instructed that a penalty will be deducted for incorrect answers, it is better to guess than to omit a question.

8) Speed tests

It is often better NOT to guess on speed tests. It has been found that on timed tests people are tempted to spend the last few seconds before time is called in marking answers at random – without even reading them – in the hope of picking up a few extra points. To discourage this practice, the instructions may warn you that your score will be "corrected" for guessing. That is, a penalty will be applied. The incorrect answers will be deducted from the correct ones, or some other penalty formula will be used.

9) Review your answers

If you finish before time is called, go back to the questions you guessed or omitted to give them further thought. Review other answers if you have time.

10) Return your test materials

If you are ready to leave before others have finished or time is called, take ALL your materials to the monitor and leave quietly. Never take any test material with you. The monitor can discover whose papers are not complete, and taking a test booklet may be grounds for disqualification.

VIII. EXAMINATION TECHNIQUES

1) Read the general instructions carefully. These are usually printed on the first page of the exam booklet. As a rule, these instructions refer to the timing of the examination; the fact that you should not start work until the signal and must stop work at a signal, etc. If there are any *special* instructions, such as a choice of questions to be answered, make sure that you note this instruction carefully.

2) When you are ready to start work on the examination, that is as soon as the signal has been given, read the instructions to each question booklet, underline any key words or phrases, such as *least, best, outline, describe* and the like. In this way you will tend to answer as requested rather than discover on reviewing your paper that you *listed without describing*, that you selected the *worst* choice rather than the *best* choice, etc.

3) If the examination is of the objective or multiple-choice type – that is, each question will also give a series of possible answers: A, B, C or D, and you are called upon to select the best answer and write the letter next to that answer on your answer paper – it is advisable to start answering each question in turn. There may be anywhere from 50 to 100 such questions in the three or four hours allotted and you can see how much time would be taken if you read through all the questions before beginning to answer any. Furthermore, if you come across a question or group of questions which you know would be difficult to answer, it would undoubtedly affect your handling of all the other questions.

4) If the examination is of the essay type and contains but a few questions, it is a moot point as to whether you should read all the questions before starting to answer any one. Of course, if you are given a choice – say five out of seven and the like – then it is essential to read all the questions so you can eliminate the two that are most difficult. If, however, you are asked to answer all the questions, there may be danger in trying to answer the easiest one first because you may find that you will spend too much time on it. The best technique is to answer the first question, then proceed to the second, etc.

5) Time your answers. Before the exam begins, write down the time it started, then add the time allowed for the examination and write down the time it must be completed, then divide the time available somewhat as follows:
   - If 3-1/2 hours are allowed, that would be 210 minutes. If you have 80 objective-type questions, that would be an average of 2-1/2 minutes per question. Allow yourself no more than 2 minutes per question, or a total of 160 minutes, which will permit about 50 minutes to review.
   - If for the time allotment of 210 minutes there are 7 essay questions to answer, that would average about 30 minutes a question. Give yourself only 25 minutes per question so that you have about 35 minutes to review.

6) The most important instruction is to *read each question* and make sure you know what is wanted. The second most important instruction is to *time yourself properly* so that you answer every question. The third most important instruction is to *answer every question.* Guess if you have to but include something for each question. Remember that you will receive no credit for a blank and will probably receive some credit if you write something in answer to an essay question. If you guess a letter – say "B" for a multiple-choice question – you may have guessed right. If you leave a blank as an answer to a multiple-choice question, the examiners may respect your feelings but it will not add a point to your score. Some exams may penalize you for wrong answers, so in such cases *only*, you may not want to guess unless you have some basis for your answer.

7) Suggestions
   a. Objective-type questions
      1. Examine the question booklet for proper sequence of pages and questions
      2. Read all instructions carefully
      3. Skip any question which seems too difficult; return to it after all other questions have been answered
      4. Apportion your time properly; do not spend too much time on any single question or group of questions

5. Note and underline key words – *all, most, fewest, least, best, worst, same, opposite,* etc.
6. Pay particular attention to negatives
7. Note unusual option, e.g., unduly long, short, complex, different or similar in content to the body of the question
8. Observe the use of "hedging" words – *probably, may, most likely,* etc.
9. Make sure that your answer is put next to the same number as the question
10. Do not second-guess unless you have good reason to believe the second answer is definitely more correct
11. Cross out original answer if you decide another answer is more accurate; do not erase until you are ready to hand your paper in
12. Answer all questions; guess unless instructed otherwise
13. Leave time for review

b. Essay questions

1. Read each question carefully
2. Determine exactly what is wanted. Underline key words or phrases.
3. Decide on outline or paragraph answer
4. Include many different points and elements unless asked to develop any one or two points or elements
5. Show impartiality by giving pros and cons unless directed to select one side only
6. Make and write down any assumptions you find necessary to answer the questions
7. Watch your English, grammar, punctuation and choice of words
8. Time your answers; don't crowd material

8) Answering the essay question

Most essay questions can be answered by framing the specific response around several key words or ideas. Here are a few such key words or ideas:

M's: manpower, materials, methods, money, management

P's: purpose, program, policy, plan, procedure, practice, problems, pitfalls, personnel, public relations

a. Six basic steps in handling problems:

1. Preliminary plan and background development
2. Collect information, data and facts
3. Analyze and interpret information, data and facts
4. Analyze and develop solutions as well as make recommendations
5. Prepare report and sell recommendations
6. Install recommendations and follow up effectiveness

b. Pitfalls to avoid

1. *Taking things for granted* – A statement of the situation does not necessarily imply that each of the elements is necessarily true; for example, a complaint may be invalid and biased so that all that can be taken for granted is that a complaint has been registered

2. *Considering only one side of a situation* – Wherever possible, indicate several alternatives and then point out the reasons you selected the best one
3. *Failing to indicate follow up* – Whenever your answer indicates action on your part, make certain that you will take proper follow-up action to see how successful your recommendations, procedures or actions turn out to be
4. *Taking too long in answering any single question* – Remember to time your answers properly

IX. AFTER THE TEST

Scoring procedures differ in detail among civil service jurisdictions although the general principles are the same. Whether the papers are hand-scored or graded by machine we have described, they are nearly always graded by number. That is, the person who marks the paper knows only the number – never the name – of the applicant. Not until all the papers have been graded will they be matched with names. If other tests, such as training and experience or oral interview ratings have been given, scores will be combined. Different parts of the examination usually have different weights. For example, the written test might count 60 percent of the final grade, and a rating of training and experience 40 percent. In many jurisdictions, veterans will have a certain number of points added to their grades.

After the final grade has been determined, the names are placed in grade order and an eligible list is established. There are various methods for resolving ties between those who get the same final grade – probably the most common is to place first the name of the person whose application was received first. Job offers are made from the eligible list in the order the names appear on it. You will be notified of your grade and your rank as soon as all these computations have been made. This will be done as rapidly as possible.

People who are found to meet the requirements in the announcement are called "eligibles." Their names are put on a list of eligible candidates. An eligible's chances of getting a job depend on how high he stands on this list and how fast agencies are filling jobs from the list.

When a job is to be filled from a list of eligibles, the agency asks for the names of people on the list of eligibles for that job. When the civil service commission receives this request, it sends to the agency the names of the three people highest on this list. Or, if the job to be filled has specialized requirements, the office sends the agency the names of the top three persons who meet these requirements from the general list.

The appointing officer makes a choice from among the three people whose names were sent to him. If the selected person accepts the appointment, the names of the others are put back on the list to be considered for future openings.

That is the rule in hiring from all kinds of eligible lists, whether they are for typist, carpenter, chemist, or something else. For every vacancy, the appointing officer has his choice of any one of the top three eligibles on the list. This explains why the person whose name is on top of the list sometimes does not get an appointment when some of the persons lower on the list do. If the appointing officer chooses the second or third eligible, the No. 1 eligible does not get a job at once, but stays on the list until he is appointed or the list is terminated.

X. HOW TO PASS THE INTERVIEW TEST

The examination for which you applied requires an oral interview test. You have already taken the written test and you are now being called for the interview test – the final part of the formal examination.

You may think that it is not possible to prepare for an interview test and that there are no procedures to follow during an interview. Our purpose is to point out some things you can do in advance that will help you and some good rules to follow and pitfalls to avoid while you are being interviewed.

What is an interview supposed to test?

The written examination is designed to test the technical knowledge and competence of the candidate; the oral is designed to evaluate intangible qualities, not readily measured otherwise, and to establish a list showing the relative fitness of each candidate – as measured against his competitors – for the position sought. Scoring is not on the basis of "right" and "wrong," but on a sliding scale of values ranging from "not passable" to "outstanding." As a matter of fact, it is possible to achieve a relatively low score without a single "incorrect" answer because of evident weakness in the qualities being measured.

Occasionally, an examination may consist entirely of an oral test – either an individual or a group oral. In such cases, information is sought concerning the technical knowledges and abilities of the candidate, since there has been no written examination for this purpose. More commonly, however, an oral test is used to supplement a written examination.

Who conducts interviews?

The composition of oral boards varies among different jurisdictions. In nearly all, a representative of the personnel department serves as chairman. One of the members of the board may be a representative of the department in which the candidate would work. In some cases, "outside experts" are used, and, frequently, a businessman or some other representative of the general public is asked to serve. Labor and management or other special groups may be represented. The aim is to secure the services of experts in the appropriate field.

However the board is composed, it is a good idea (and not at all improper or unethical) to ascertain in advance of the interview who the members are and what groups they represent. When you are introduced to them, you will have some idea of their backgrounds and interests, and at least you will not stutter and stammer over their names.

What should be done before the interview?

While knowledge about the board members is useful and takes some of the surprise element out of the interview, there is other preparation which is more substantive. It *is* possible to prepare for an oral interview – in several ways:

1) Keep a copy of your application and review it carefully before the interview

This may be the only document before the oral board, and the starting point of the interview. Know what education and experience you have listed there, and the sequence and dates of all of it. Sometimes the board will ask you to review the highlights of your experience for them; you should not have to hem and haw doing it.

2) Study the class specification and the examination announcement

Usually, the oral board has one or both of these to guide them. The qualities, characteristics or knowledges required by the position sought are stated in these documents. They offer valuable clues as to the nature of the oral interview. For example, if the job involves supervisory responsibilities, the announcement will usually indicate that knowledge of modern supervisory methods and the qualifications of the candidate as a supervisor will be tested. If so, you can expect such questions, frequently in the form of a hypothetical situation which you are expected to solve. NEVER go into an oral without knowledge of the duties and responsibilities of the job you seek.

3) Think through each qualification required

Try to visualize the kind of questions you would ask if you were a board member. How well could you answer them? Try especially to appraise your own knowledge and background in each area, *measured against the job sought*, and identify any areas in which you are weak. Be critical and realistic – do not flatter yourself.

4) Do some general reading in areas in which you feel you may be weak

For example, if the job involves supervision and your past experience has NOT, some general reading in supervisory methods and practices, particularly in the field of human relations, might be useful. Do NOT study agency procedures or detailed manuals. The oral board will be testing your understanding and capacity, not your memory.

5) Get a good night's sleep and watch your general health and mental attitude

You will want a clear head at the interview. Take care of a cold or any other minor ailment, and of course, no hangovers.

What should be done on the day of the interview?

Now comes the day of the interview itself. Give yourself plenty of time to get there. Plan to arrive somewhat ahead of the scheduled time, particularly if your appointment is in the fore part of the day. If a previous candidate fails to appear, the board might be ready for you a bit early. By early afternoon an oral board is almost invariably behind schedule if there are many candidates, and you may have to wait. Take along a book or magazine to read, or your application to review, but leave any extraneous material in the waiting room when you go in for your interview. In any event, relax and compose yourself.

The matter of dress is important. The board is forming impressions about you – from your experience, your manners, your attitude, and your appearance. Give your personal appearance careful attention. Dress your best, but not your flashiest. Choose conservative, appropriate clothing, and be sure it is immaculate. This is a business interview, and your appearance should indicate that you regard it as such. Besides, being well groomed and properly dressed will help boost your confidence.

Sooner or later, someone will call your name and escort you into the interview room. *This is it.* From here on you are on your own. It is too late for any more preparation. But remember, you asked for this opportunity to prove your fitness, and you are here because your request was granted.

What happens when you go in?

The usual sequence of events will be as follows: The clerk (who is often the board stenographer) will introduce you to the chairman of the oral board, who will introduce you to the other members of the board. Acknowledge the introductions before you sit down. Do not be surprised if you find a microphone facing you or a stenotypist sitting by. Oral interviews are usually recorded in the event of an appeal or other review.

Usually the chairman of the board will open the interview by reviewing the highlights of your education and work experience from your application – primarily for the benefit of the other members of the board, as well as to get the material into the record. Do not interrupt or comment unless there is an error or significant misinterpretation; if that is the case, do not hesitate. But do not quibble about insignificant matters. Also, he will usually ask you some question about your education, experience or your present job – partly to get you to start talking and to establish the interviewing "rapport." He may start the actual questioning, or turn it over to one of the other members. Frequently, each member undertakes the questioning on a particular area, one in which he is perhaps most competent, so you can expect each member to participate in the examination. Because time is limited, you may also expect some rather abrupt switches in the direction the questioning takes, so do not be upset by it. Normally, a board member will not pursue a single line of questioning unless he discovers a particular strength or weakness.

After each member has participated, the chairman will usually ask whether any member has any further questions, then will ask you if you have anything you wish to add. Unless you are expecting this question, it may floor you. Worse, it may start you off on an extended, extemporaneous speech. The board is not usually seeking more information. The question is principally to offer you a last opportunity to present further qualifications or to indicate that you have nothing to add. So, if you feel that a significant qualification or characteristic has been overlooked, it is proper to point it out in a sentence or so. Do not compliment the board on the thoroughness of their examination – they have been sketchy, and you know it. If you wish, merely say, "No thank you, I have nothing further to add." This is a point where you can "talk yourself out" of a good impression or fail to present an important bit of information. Remember, *you close the interview yourself.*

The chairman will then say, "That is all, Mr. ______, thank you." Do not be startled; the interview is over, and quicker than you think. Thank him, gather your belongings and take your leave. Save your sigh of relief for the other side of the door.

How to put your best foot forward

Throughout this entire process, you may feel that the board individually and collectively is trying to pierce your defenses, seek out your hidden weaknesses and embarrass and confuse you. Actually, this is not true. They are obliged to make an appraisal of your qualifications for the job you are seeking, and they want to see you in your best light. Remember, they must interview all candidates and a non-cooperative candidate may become a failure in spite of their best efforts to bring out his qualifications. Here are 15 suggestions that will help you:

1) Be natural – Keep your attitude confident, not cocky

If you are not confident that you can do the job, do not expect the board to be. Do not apologize for your weaknesses, try to bring out your strong points. The board is interested in a positive, not negative, presentation. Cockiness will antagonize any board member and make him wonder if you are covering up a weakness by a false show of strength.

2) Get comfortable, but don't lounge or sprawl

Sit erectly but not stiffly. A careless posture may lead the board to conclude that you are careless in other things, or at least that you are not impressed by the importance of the occasion. Either conclusion is natural, even if incorrect. Do not fuss with your clothing, a pencil or an ashtray. Your hands may occasionally be useful to emphasize a point; do not let them become a point of distraction.

3) Do not wisecrack or make small talk

This is a serious situation, and your attitude should show that you consider it as such. Further, the time of the board is limited – they do not want to waste it, and neither should you.

4) Do not exaggerate your experience or abilities

In the first place, from information in the application or other interviews and sources, the board may know more about you than you think. Secondly, you probably will not get away with it. An experienced board is rather adept at spotting such a situation, so do not take the chance.

5) If you know a board member, do not make a point of it, yet do not hide it

Certainly you are not fooling him, and probably not the other members of the board. Do not try to take advantage of your acquaintanceship – it will probably do you little good.

6) Do not dominate the interview

Let the board do that. They will give you the clues – do not assume that you have to do all the talking. Realize that the board has a number of questions to ask you, and do not try to take up all the interview time by showing off your extensive knowledge of the answer to the first one.

7) Be attentive

You only have 20 minutes or so, and you should keep your attention at its sharpest throughout. When a member is addressing a problem or question to you, give him your undivided attention. Address your reply principally to him, but do not exclude the other board members.

8) Do not interrupt

A board member may be stating a problem for you to analyze. He will ask you a question when the time comes. Let him state the problem, and wait for the question.

9) Make sure you understand the question

Do not try to answer until you are sure what the question is. If it is not clear, restate it in your own words or ask the board member to clarify it for you. However, do not haggle about minor elements.

10) Reply promptly but not hastily

A common entry on oral board rating sheets is "candidate responded readily," or "candidate hesitated in replies." Respond as promptly and quickly as you can, but do not jump to a hasty, ill-considered answer.

11) Do not be peremptory in your answers

A brief answer is proper – but do not fire your answer back. That is a losing game from your point of view. The board member can probably ask questions much faster than you can answer them.

12) Do not try to create the answer you think the board member wants

He is interested in what kind of mind you have and how it works – not in playing games. Furthermore, he can usually spot this practice and will actually grade you down on it.

13) Do not switch sides in your reply merely to agree with a board member

Frequently, a member will take a contrary position merely to draw you out and to see if you are willing and able to defend your point of view. Do not start a debate, yet do not surrender a good position. If a position is worth taking, it is worth defending.

14) Do not be afraid to admit an error in judgment if you are shown to be wrong

The board knows that you are forced to reply without any opportunity for careful consideration. Your answer may be demonstrably wrong. If so, admit it and get on with the interview.

15) Do not dwell at length on your present job

The opening question may relate to your present assignment. Answer the question but do not go into an extended discussion. You are being examined for a *new* job, not your present one. As a matter of fact, try to phrase ALL your answers in terms of the job for which you are being examined.

Basis of Rating

Probably you will forget most of these "do's" and "don'ts" when you walk into the oral interview room. Even remembering them all will not ensure you a passing grade. Perhaps you did not have the qualifications in the first place. But remembering them will help you to put your best foot forward, without treading on the toes of the board members.

Rumor and popular opinion to the contrary notwithstanding, an oral board wants you to make the best appearance possible. They know you are under pressure – but they also want to see how you respond to it as a guide to what your reaction would be under the pressures of the job you seek. They will be influenced by the degree of poise you display, the personal traits you show and the manner in which you respond.

ABOUT THIS BOOK

This book contains tests divided into Examination Sections. Go through each test, answering every question in the margin. We have also attached a sample answer sheet at the back of the book that can be removed and used. At the end of each test look at the answer key and check your answers. On the ones you got wrong, look at the right answer choice and learn. Do not fill in the answers first. Do not memorize the questions and answers, but understand the answer and principles involved. On your test, the questions will likely be different from the samples. Questions are changed and new ones added. If you understand these past questions you should have success with any changes that arise. Tests may consist of several types of questions. We have additional books on each subject should more study be advisable or necessary for you. Finally, the more you study, the better prepared you will be. This book is intended to be the last thing you study before you walk into the examination room. Prior study of relevant texts is also recommended. NLC publishes some of these in our Fundamental Series. Knowledge and good sense are important factors in passing your exam. Good luck also helps. So now study this Passbook, absorb the material contained within and take that knowledge into the examination. Then do your best to pass that exam.

EXAMINATION SECTION

EXAMINATION SECTION
TEST 1

DIRECTIONS: Each question or incomplete statement is followed by several suggested answers or completions. Select the one that BEST answers the question or completes the statement. *PRINT THE LETTER OF THE CORRECT ANSWER IN THE SPACE AT THE RIGHT.*

Questions 1-5.

DIRECTIONS: Questions 1 through 5 are to be answered on the basis of the following statement. Use ONLY the information contained in this statement in answering these questions.

No multiple dwelling shall be erected to a height in excess of one and one-half times the width of the widest street on which it faces, except that above the level of such height, for each one foot that the front wall of such dwelling sets back from the street line, three feet shall be added to the height limit of such dwelling, but such dwelling shall not exceed in maximum height three feet plus one and three-quarter times the width of the widest street on which it faces.

Any such dwelling facing a street more than one hundred feet in width shall be subject to the same height limitations as though such dwelling faced a street one hundred feet in width.

1. The MAXIMUM height of a multiple dwelling set back five feet from the street line and facing a 60 foot wide street is ______ feet. 1.____

   A. 60 B. 90 C. 105 D. 165

2. The MAXIMUM height of a multiple dwelling set back six feet from the street line and facing a 120 foot wide street is ______ feet. 2.____

   A. 198 B. 168 C. 120 D. 105

3. The MAXIMUM height of a multiple dwelling is 3.____

   A. 100 ft. B. 150 ft. C. 178 ft. D. unlimited

4. The MAXIMUM height of a multiple dwelling set back 10 feet from the street line and facing a 110 foot wide street is ______ feet. 4.____

   A. 178 B. 180 C. 195 D. 205

5. The MAXIMUM height of a multiple dwelling set back eight feet from the street line and facing a 90 foot wide street is ______ feet. 5.____

   A. 135 B. 147 C. 178 D. 159

Questions 6-10.

DIRECTIONS: Questions 6 through 10 are to be answered on the basis of the following statement. Use ONLY the information contained in this statement in answering these questions.

The number of persons accommodated on any story in a lodging house shall not be greater than the sum of the following components.

a. 22 persons for each full multiple of 22 inches in the smallest clear width for each means of egress approved by the department, other than fire escapes.
b. 20 persons for each lawful fire escape accessible from such story.

6. The MAXIMUM number of persons that may be accommodated on a story in a lodging house depends on the 6.____

A. number of lawful fire escapes *only*
B. number of approved means of egress *only*
C. smallest clear width in each approved means of egress *only*
D. number of lawful fire escapes and sum total of smallest clear widths in each approved means of egress

7. The MAXIMUM number of persons that may be accommodated on a story of a lodging house having one lawful fire escape and a sum total of 44 inches in the smallest clear widths of the two approved means of egress is 7.____

A. 20 B. 22 C. 42 D. 64

8. The MAXIMUM number of persons that may be accommodated on a story of a lodging house having two lawful fire escapes and a sum total of 60 inches in the smallest clear width of the approved means of egress is 8.____

A. 64 B. 84 C. 100 D. 106

9. The MAXIMUM number of persons that may be accommodated on a story of a lodging house having one lawful fire escape and a sum total of 33 inches in the smallest clear width of the approved means of egress is 9.____

A. 42 B. 53 C. 64 D. 73

10. The MAXIMUM number of persons that may be accommodated on a story of a lodging house having two lawful fire escapes and two approved means of egress, with 40 inches and 44 inches in the smallest clear widths, respectively, is 10.____

A. 84 B. 104 C. 106 D. 108

11. An employee of the Department of Housing and Buildings may take outside employment in private industry as a(n) 11.____

A. architect B. mason
C. plumber D. none of the above

12. The one of the following that is NOT a multiple dwelling is a 12.____

A. college dormitory
B. dwelling occupied by three families
C. hospital
D. lodging house

13. The one of the following that is a Class A multiple dwelling is a 13.____

A. commercial building containing a janitor's apartment
B. furnished room house

C. hotel
D. tenement

14. A dwelling occupied by one family with five transient roomers is a ______ dwelling. 14.____

A. Class A multiple
B. Class B multiple
C. single family private
D. two-family private

15. The one of the following that is deemed a living room by the multiple dwelling law is a 15.____

A. bathroom
B. bedroom
C. dinette, 45 sq. ft. in area
D. kitchenette, 45 sq. ft. in area

16. The MAXIMUM number of stories to which a new multiple dwelling may be erected without having a passenger elevator is 16.____

A. 4
B. 5
C. 6
D. 7

17. In a new multiple dwelling, which of the following rooms are required to have windows? 17.____

A. Bathroom
B. Kitchen
C. Water-closet compartment
D. All of the above

18. New multiple dwellings three stories or more in height must have hot water supplied during 18.____

A. the hours between 6 A.M. and Midnight *only*
B. the hours between 8 A.M. and 8 P.M. *only*
C. the hours between 6 A.M. and Noon and 6 P.M. and Midnight *only*
D. all hours

19. A winding stair in a new multiple dwelling is 19.____

A. not permitted under any circumstances
B. permitted under all circumstances
C. permitted only when the building is more than 6 stories high
D. permitted only when the building is less than 6 stories high

20. All elevator shaft walls in new multiple dwellings MUST be 20.____

A. at least 4 inches thick
B. fireproof
C. hollow
D. made of gypsum plaster

21. The one of the following statements about new multiple dwellings that is NOT true is: 21.____

A. Boiler rooms in multiple dwellings four stories or more in height must have fireproof doors
B. Every open roof area must have a guard rail or parapet wall at least 3'6" high
C. A new multiple dwelling may be placed on the same lot with a frame building
D. A new multiple dwelling may be used for parking of passenger motor vehicles

22. A tenement within the meaning of the multiple dwelling law is a building erected BEFORE 22.____

A. April 18, 1929
B. April 6, 1948
C. April 12, 1949
D. March 25, 1952

23. Every entrance hall in a multiple dwelling must be provided with a light of AT LEAST _______ watts. 23.____

A. 5
B. 10
C. 15
D. 40

24. From the entrance to the first stair, every entrance hall in a new multiple dwelling must be, in clear width, AT LEAST 24.____

A. 3'8"
B. 4'
C. 6'
D. 8'

25. A basement in a new multiple dwelling exceeding seven stories in height MUST have AT LEAST one-half of its height _______ curb level and is _______ as a story. 25.____

A. above; counted
B. above; not counted
C. below; counted
D. below; not counted

26. The lower ends of mitred cross bridging should be nailed to the beams 26.____

A. at the same time that the top ends are nailed
B. before the rough flooring is placed
C. after the plastering is complete
D. after the flooring is placed

27. The maximum distance between lines of bridging should NOT exceed 27.____

A. 10'0"
B. 8'0"
C. 6'6"
D. 4'6"

28. The building code states that it shall be unlawful to corbel walls less than twelve inches thick, except for fire-stopping.
From this, it may be concluded that 28.____

A. walls 12 inches or more in thickness shall not be corbelled
B. if a wall is less than 12 inches thick, it is permissible to corbel provided some of the corbelling is used for fire-stopping
C. fire-stopping shall not be considered to be corbelling
D. corbelling and fire-stopping are the same

29. The building code states that curtain walls of solid masonry shall be at least eight inches thick for the uppermost thirteen feet and at least twelve inches thick for the next fifty-two feet or fraction thereof below and shall be increased four inches in thickness for each succeeding sixty feet or fraction thereof below.
This means that the thickness of a solid masonry curtain wall 126 feet high should be AT LEAST 29.____

A. 20 inches throughout its height
B. 20 inches at the base
C. 16 inches throughout its height
D. 16 inches at the base

30. The term *curb cut* refers to 30.____

A. openings in a curb
B. tire cuts made while parking
C. surveying marks chiseled in a curb
D. rental for sidewalk stands

31. A bearing wall is a wall which 31.____

A. carries its own weight *only*
B. carries load other than its own weight
C. bears on structural supports at each story
D. is more than 12 feet high

32. A column is an ______ member. 32.____

A. upright compression
B. inclined compression
C. upright tension
D. inclined tension

33. A lintel could be broadly classified as a 33.____

A. beam B. column C. footing D. strut

34. A flat slab is MOST commonly used in ______ construction. 34.____

A. sidewalk B. roadway C. conduit D. building

35. Of the following, the member which would MOST likely be supported on a footing is the 35.____

A. beam B. girder C. column D. joist

36. A parapet wall would MOST likely support 36.____

A. a coping
B. roof joists
C. floor joists
D. partitions

37. Jack arches are used 37.____

A. in ornamental iron work
B. in fancy stairways
C. when lintels are omitted
D. in foundations

38. If green lumber is used for joists, shrinkage will have its MOST serious effect in ______ of joists. 38.____

A. length B. width C. depth D. weight

39. The phrase *concealed draft openings* is MOST likely to be used in connection with 39.____

A. fireplaces
B. flues
C. fire-stopping
D. automatic dampers

40. Of the following terms, the one which is LEAST related to the others is the 40.____

A. jamb
B. strike plate
C. latch bolt
D. pulley stile

Questions 41-45.

DIRECTIONS: Questions 41 through 45 are to be answered in accordance with the following sketch.

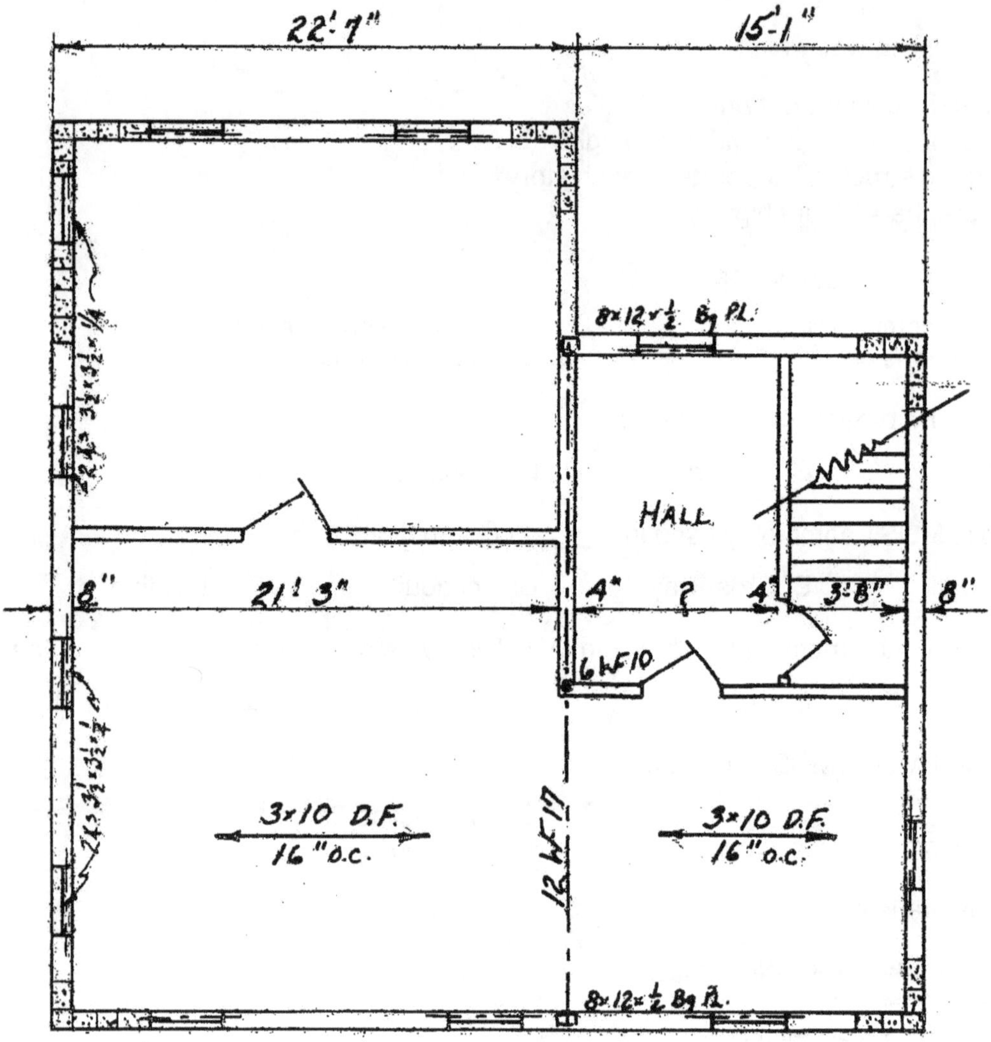

2ND FL. PLAN

41. The one of the following statements that is CORRECT is: The building 41.____

A. is of fireproof construction
B. has masonry walls, with wood joists
C. is of wood frame construction
D. has timber posts and girders

42. The one of the following statements that is CORRECT is: 42.____

A. The stairway from the ground floor continues through the roof
B. There are two means of egress from the second floor of this building
C. The door on the second floor stair landing opens in the direction of egress
D. The entire stair is shown on this plan

43. The width of the hall is 43.____

A. 10'3" B. 10'5" C. 10'7" D. 10'9"

44. The lintels shown are 44.____

A. angles B. a channel and an angle
C. an I-beam D. precast concrete

45. The one of the following statements that is CORRECT is: The steel beam is 45.____

A. supported by columns at the center and at the ends
B. entirely supported by the walls
C. supported on columns at the ends only
D. supported at the center by a column and at the ends by the walls

---

KEY (CORRECT ANSWERS)

1. C	11. D	21. C	31. B	41. B
2. B	12. C	22. A	32. A	42. C
3. C	13. D	23. C	33. A	43. D
4. A	14. B	24. B	34. D	44. A
5. D	15. B	25. A	35. C	45. D
6. D	16. C	26. D	36. A	
7. D	17. D	27. B	37. C	
8. B	18. A	28. C	38. C	
9. A	19. A	29. B	39. C	
10. C	20. B	30. A	40. D	

EVALUATING INFORMATION AND EVIDENCE

EXAMINATION SECTION

TEST 1

DIRECTIONS: Each question or incomplete statement is followed by several suggested answers or completions. Select the one that BEST answers the question or completes the statement. *PRINT THE LETTER OF THE CORRECT ANSWER IN THE SPACE AT THE RIGHT.*

Question 1-4.

DIRECTIONS: Questions 1 through 4 measure your ability (1) to determine whether statements from witnesses say essentially the same thing and (2) to determine the evidence needed to make it reasonably certain that a particular conclusion is true.

To do well in this part of the test, you do NOT have to have a working knowledge of police procedures and techniques or to have any more familiarity with crimes and criminal behavior than that acquired from reading newspapers, listening to radio, or watching TV. In order to do well in this part, you must read carefully and reason closely. Sloppy reading or sloppy reasoning will lead to a low score.

1. In which of the following do the two statements made say essentially the same thing in two different ways? 1.____
   I. All members of the pro-x group are free from persecution.
   No person that is persecuted is a member of the pro-x group.
   II. Some responsible employees of the police department are not supervisors.
   Some police department supervisors are not responsible employees.

   The CORRECT answer is:
   A. I only
   B. II only
   C. Both I and II
   D. Neither I nor II

2. In which the following do the two statements made say essentially the same thing in two different ways? 2.____
   I. All Nassau County police officers weigh less than 225 pounds.
   No police officer weighs more than 225 pounds.
   II. No police officer is an alcoholic.
   No alcoholic is a police officer.

   The CORRECT answer is:
   A. I only
   B. II only
   C. Both I and II
   D. Neither I nor II

3. <u>Summary of Evidence Collected to Date</u>: All pimps in the precinct own pink-colored cars and carry knives. 3.____
   <u>Prematurely Drawn Conclusion</u>: Any person in the precinct who carries a knife is a pimp.

Which one of the following additional pieces of evidence, if any, would make it *reasonably certain* that the conclusion drawn is TRUE?

A. Each person who carries a knife owns a pink-colored car.
B. All persons who own pink-colored cars pimp.
C. No one who carries a knife has a vocation other than pimping.
D. None of the above

4. Summary of Evidence Collected to Date: 4.____

a. Some of the robbery suspects have served time as convicted felons.
b. Some of the robbery suspects are female.

Prematurely Drawn Conclusion: Some of the female suspects have never served time as convicted felons.

Which one of the following additional pieces of evidence, if any, would make it *reasonably certain* that the conclusion drawn is TRUE?

A. The number of female suspects is the same as the number of robber suspects who have served time as convicted felons.
B. The number of female suspects is smaller than the number of convicted felons.
C. The number of suspects that have served time is smaller than the number of suspects that have been convicted of a felony.
D. None of the above

Questions 5-8.

DIRECTIONS: Questions 5 through 8 measure your ability to orient yourself within a given section of a town, neighborhood, or particular area. Each of the questions describes a starting point and a destination. Assume that you are driving a patrol car in the area shown on the map accompanying the questions. Use the map as a basis for choosing the shortest way to get from one point to another without breaking the law.

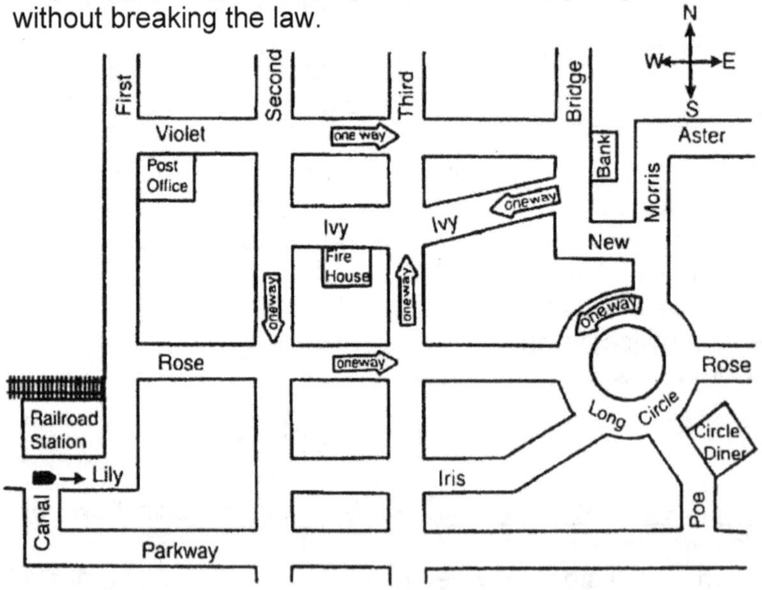

A street marked one way is one-way for the full length, even when there are breaks or jogs in the street. EXCEPTION: A street that does not have the same name over the full length.

5. A patrol car at the train station is sent to the bank to investigate a robbery. The SHORTEST way to get there without breaking any traffic laws is to go 5.____
   A. east on Lily, north on First, east on Rose, north on Third, and east on Ivy to bank
   B. east on Lily, north on First, east on Violet, and south on Bridge to bank
   C. south on Canal, east on Parkway, north on Poe, around Long Circle to Morris, west on New, and north on Bridge to bank
   D. south on Canal, east on Parkway, north on Third, and east on Ivy to bank

6. At the bank, the patrol car receives a call to hurry to the post office. The SHORTEST way to get there without breaking any traffic laws is to go 6.____
   A. west on Ivy, south on Second, west on Rose, and north on First to post office
   B. west on Ivy, south on Second, west on Rose, and south on First to post office
   C. south on Bridge, east on New, south on Morris, around Long Circle, south on Poe, west on Parkway, north on Canal, east on Lily, and north on First to post office
   D. north on Bridge, west on Violet, and south on First to post office

7. On leaving the post office, the police officers decide to go to the Circle Diner. The SHORTEST way to get there without breaking any traffic laws is to go 7.____
   A. south on First, left on Rose, right on Second, left on Parkway, and right on Poe to diner
   B. south on First, left on Rose, around Long Circle, and right on Poe to diner
   C. south on First, left on Rose, right on Second, right on Iris, around Long Circle, and left on Poe to diner
   D. west on Violet, right on Bridge, right on new, right on Morris, around Long Circle, and left on Poe to diner

8. During lunch break, a fire siren sounds and the police officers rush to their patrol car and head to the firehouse. The SHORTEST way to get there without breaking any traffic laws is to go 8.____
   A. north on Poe, around Long Circle, west on Iris, north on Third, and west on Ivy to firehouse
   B. north on Poe, around Long Circle,, north on Morris, west on New, north on Bridge, and west on Ivy to firehouse
   C. north on Poe, around Long Circle, west on Rose, north on Third, and west on Ivy to firehouse
   D. south on Poe, west on Parkway, north on Third, and east on Ivy to firehouse

Questions 9-13.

DIRECTIONS: Questions 9 through 13 measure your ability to understand written descriptions of events. Each question presents you with a description of an accident, a crime, or an event and asks you which of four drawings BEST represent it.

In the drawings, the following symbols are used (these symbols and their meanings will be repeated in the test):

A moving vehicle is represented by this symbol: (front) (rear)

A parked vehicle is represented by this symbol: (front) (rear)

A pedestrian or a bicyclist is represented by this symbol: •

The path and direction of travel of a vehicle or pedestrian is indicated by a solid line: ⟶

EXCEPTION: The path and direction of travel of each vehicle or person directly involved in a collision from the point of impact is indicated by a dotted line: - - →

9. A driver pulling out from between two parked cars on Magic is struck by a vehicle heading east which turns left onto Maple and flees. 9.____
Which of the following depicts the accident?

A.

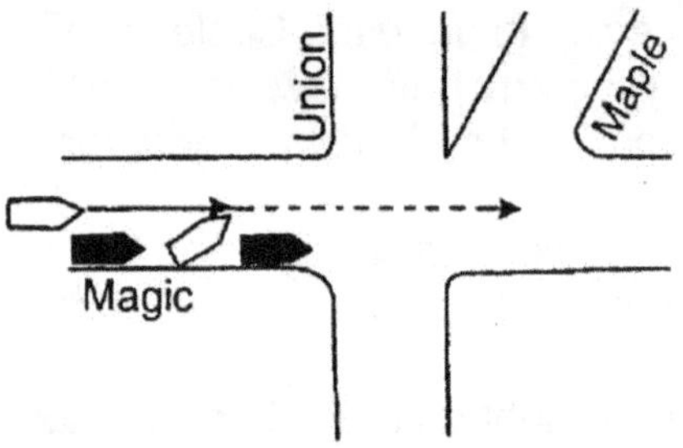

B.

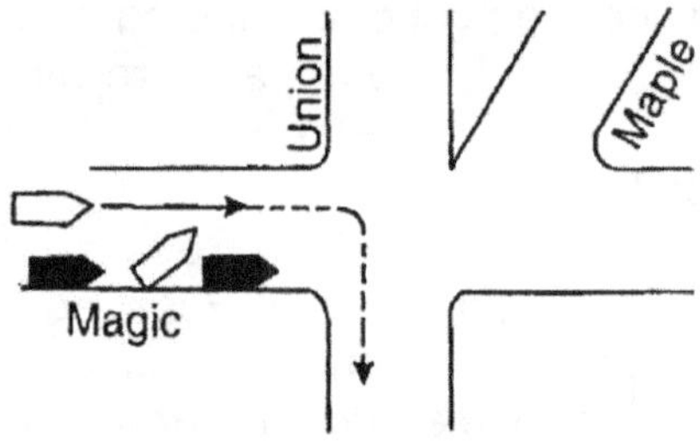

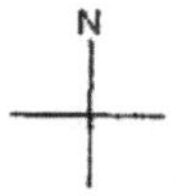

C.

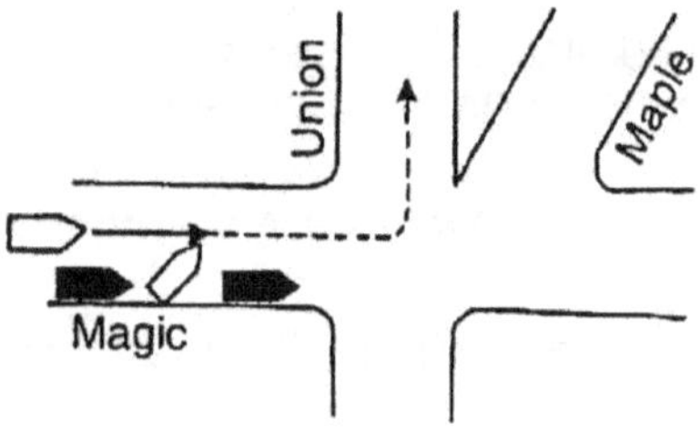

D.

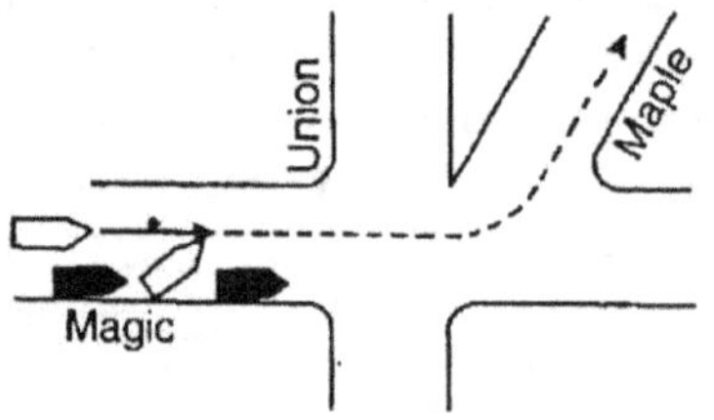

10. As Mr. Jones is driving south on Side St., he falls asleep at the wheel. His car goes out of control and sideswipes an oncoming car, goes through an intersection, and hits a pedestrian on the southeast corner of Main Street. Which of the following depicts the accident? 10.____

A.

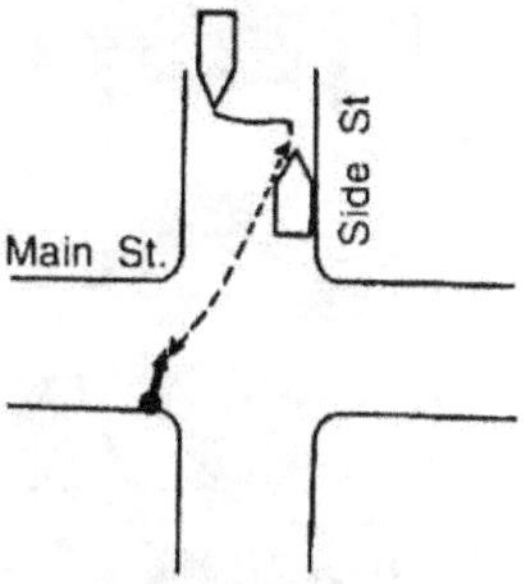

B.

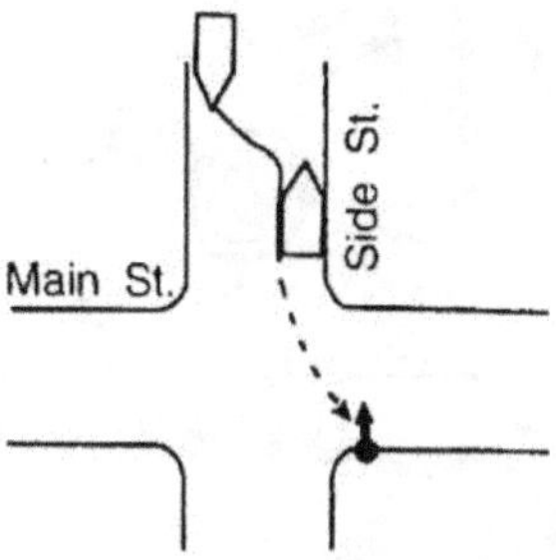

C.

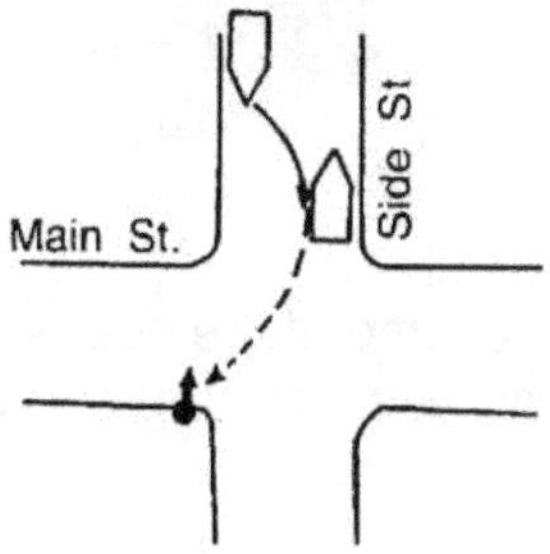

D.

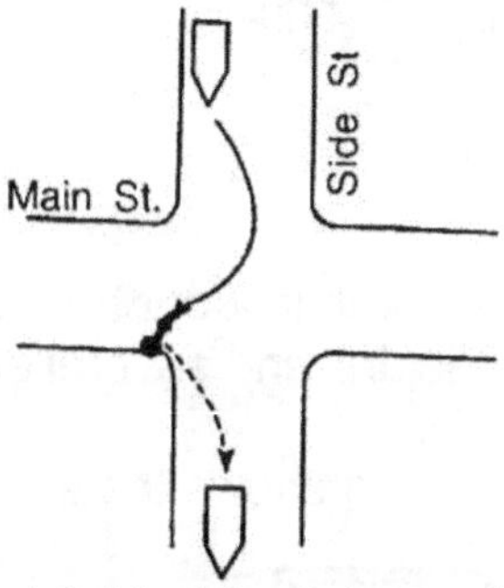

11. A car traveling south on Baltic skids through a red light at the intersection of Baltic and Atlantic, sideswipes a car stopped for a light in the northbound lane, skids 180 degrees, and stops on the west sidewalk of Baltic. Which of the following depicts the accident? 11.____

A.

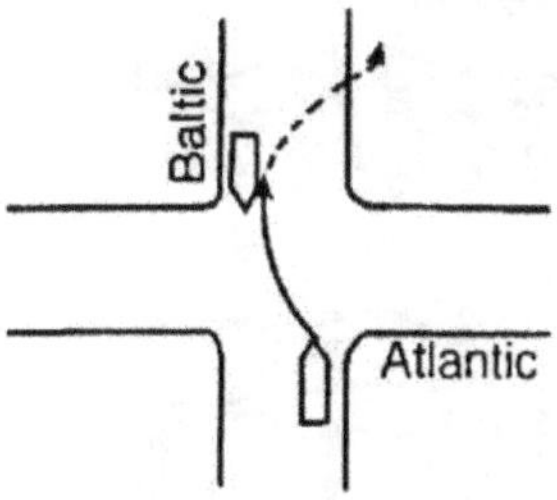

B.

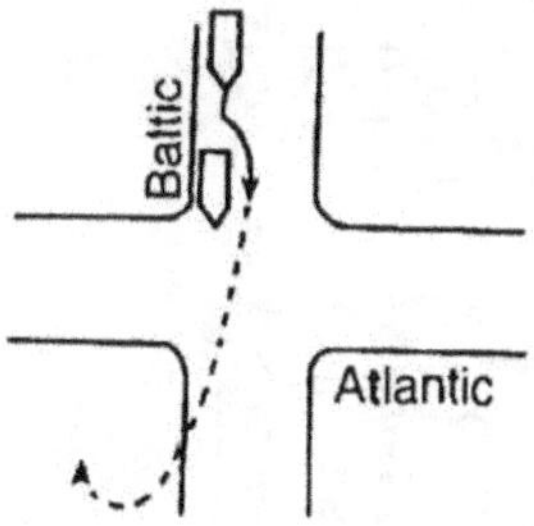

C.

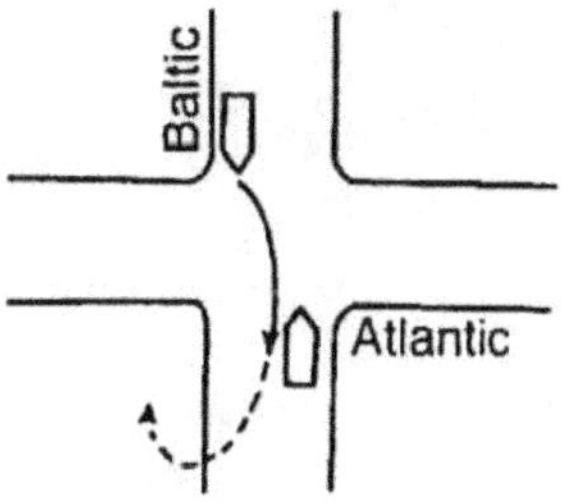

D.

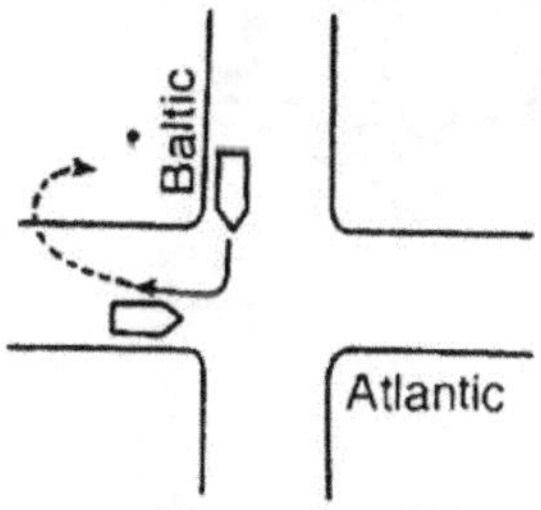

12. When found, the right front end of an automobile was smashed and bent around a post, and the hood was buckled.
Which of the following cars on a service lot is the car described? 12.____

A.

B.

C.

D.

13. An open floor safe with its door bet out of shape was found at the scene. It was empty. An electric drill and several envelopes and papers were found on the floor near the safe.
Which of the following shows the scene described? 13.____

A.

B.

C.

D.

Questions 14-16.

DIRECTIONS: In Questions 14 through 16, you are to pick the word or phrase CLOSEST in meaning to the word or phrase printed in capital letters.

14. HAZARDOUS 14.____
A. uncertain B. threatening C. difficult D. dangerous

15. NEGLIGENT 15.____
A. careless B. fearless C. ruthless D. useless

16. PROVOKE 16.____
A. accuse B. arouse C. insist D. suspend

Questions 17-20.

DIRECTIONS: Questions 17 through 20 measure your ability to do arithmetic related to police work. Each question presents a separate arithmetic problem to be solved.

17. To the nearest hour, how long can a specialized police vehicle with a 40-gallon fuel tank be on the road before heading for a service facility, assuming that the vehicle consumes 8 gallons per hour and must head for a service facility when there are only 8 gallons in the tank? 17.____
A. 3 B. 4 C. 5 D. None of the above

18. A man with a history of vagrancy was found dead under a bridge with the following U.S. currency in a band around his belly: 18.____
7 $5 bills, 3 $10 bills, 11 $20 bills, 9 $50 bills, 4 $100 bills
What is the TOTAL amount of the money that was found in the band?
A. $1,015 B. $1,135 C. $2,719 D. None of the above

19. X is 110 dimes; Y is 1,111 pennies. 19.____
Which of the following statements about the values of X and Y above is TRUE?
A. X is greater than Y.
B. Y is greater than X.
C. x equals Y.
D. The relationship of X to Y cannot be determined from the information given.

20. Which of the following individuals drinking hard liquor in a bar was 21 years old at the time of the incident? 20.____
A. One born August 26, 1989. Date of incident is March 17, 2010.
B. One born January 6, 1989. Date of incident is New Year's Eve 2009.
C. One born 3/17/89. Date of incident is 2/14/10
D. None of the above

KEY (CORRECT ANSWERS)

1.	A	11.	C
2.	B	12.	D
3.	C	13.	B
4.	D	14.	D
5.	B	15.	A
6.	C	16.	B
7.	B	17.	B
8.	B	18.	B
9.	D	19.	B
10.	B	20.	D

LOGICAL REASONING
EVALUATING CONCLUSIONS IN LIGHT OF KNOWN FACTS

EXAMINATION SECTION
TEST 1

DIRECTIONS: For the following questions, select the letter before the statement below which BEST expresses the relationship between the facts and the conclusion. Mark your answer:

A. The facts prove the conclusion; or
B. The facts disprove the conclusion; or
C. The facts neither prove nor disprove the conclusion.

PRINT THE LETTER OF THE CORRECT ANSWER IN THE SPACE AT THE RIGHT.

1. FACTS: Andy types half as fast as Bill. Bill types twice as slow as Charlie. Bill types 60 words a minute. 1.____

   CONCLUSION: Charlie types 30 words a minute.

2. FACTS: If Albert gets traded to the Cubs, Chris will have to be traded to the Padres. Albert will avoid being traded only if he hits a home run in his turn at bat. If Chris goes to the Padres, Dave will be traded to the Dodgers. Albert strikes out in this crucial at-bat. 2.____

   CONCLUSION: Dave gets traded to the Dodgers.

3. FACTS: All beads are forms of jewelry. All jewelry is expensive. Everyone loves expensive beads. 3.____

   CONCLUSION: All beads are expensive.

4. FACTS: No shrimp are mussels. Mussels are bivalves. All mussels have shells. 4.____

   CONCLUSION: Therefore, no shrimp have shells.

5. FACTS: On their latest diet, Abby, Bea, Celia, and Donna lost a combined total of 260 pounds. Abby lost twice as much as Celia. Celia lost half as much as the woman who lost the most. Donna lost 80 pounds. 5.____

   CONCLUSION: Abby lost 100 pounds; Bea, 30; Celia, 50; and Donna, 80.

6. FACTS: Ann's office is two floors above Brenda's. Brenda's office is one floor below the only woman in the building whose birthday is today. Sally's office is on the third floor. Ann's office is on the fourth floor. 6.____

   CONCLUSION: Today is Ann's birthday.

7. FACTS: Douglas Ave. is perpendicular to Bates St. Bates St. is parallel to Adams Ave. Douglas Ave. is parallel to Charles St. Evans Ave. is parallel to the streets that are perpendicular to Bates St. 7.____

   CONCLUSION: Evans Ave. is perpendicular to Douglas Ave.

8. FACTS: There's one out, and Bill is the runner on third base. If Arnie hits the ball hard, Bill will run, but so slowly that he will be out at home plate. The team captain, on second base, will not run unless Arnie hits the ball hard. The captain runs. 8.____

CONCLUSION: Bill is safe.

9. FACTS: Some members of this genus are members of that species. All members of that species are butterflies. Some butterflies are different from others. 9.____

CONCLUSION: Some members of this genus are butterflies.

10. FACTS: Some woodwinds are clarinets. Flutes are not clarinets. All clarinets are beautiful things. 10.____

CONCLUSION: Therefore, all beautiful things are woodwinds.

11. FACTS: Using a grid exactly like the one below, Joe Genius filled in the numbers 1 through 9 in the boxes. Each horizontal, vertical, and diagonal row added up to 15. A different number went in each box. 11.____

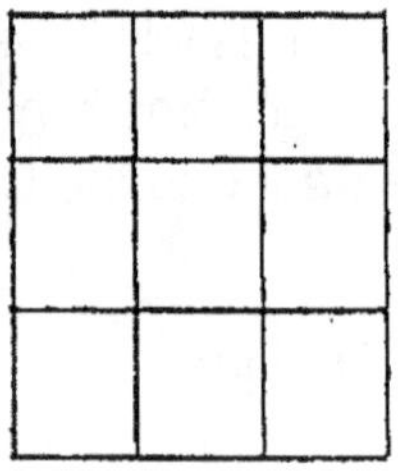

CONCLUSION: The number Joe put in the middle box was 6.

12. FACTS: Max, Nick, Pete, and Ollie all bought different colored suits: grey, green, blue, and brown, but not necessarily respectively. Max paid less for his green suit than Nick paid for his suit. Ollie paid twice what Pete paid. Pete paid the same as the man who bought the grey suit. Ollie bought the brown suit. 12.____

CONCLUSION: Ollie paid the most.

13. FACTS: Four people (Alice, Bob, Carol, and Dave) are sitting at a square table, discussing their favorite sports. Bob sits directly across from the jogger. Carol sits to the right of the basketball player. Alice sits across from Dave. The golfer sits to the left of the tennis player. A man sits on Dave's right. 13.____

CONCLUSION: Dave plays golf.

14. FACTS: An employer decided to offer a job to everyone who scored higher than 50 on an exam. Alice scored 20. Betty scored lower than Carol, but more than twice as high as Alice. 14.____

CONCLUSION: Of the three women, only Carol was offered the job.

15. FACTS: If Camille's squirrel has rabies and the squirrel bites Casey's cat, the squirrel will have to be caught and the cat will get rabies. If the cat has had rabies shots within the last two years, the cat will not get rabies. Casey's cat did not get rabies. 15.____

CONCLUSION: Casey's cat has had rabies shots within the last two years.

16. FACTS: Sally will file a grievance only if Bill fires her. If Laura tells Frank the whole story, Frank will tell it to Bill. If Bill hears the whole story, he will not fire Sally. Laura tells Fred the whole story. 16.____

CONCLUSION: Sally files a grievance.

17. FACTS: If Alice leaves work early, Barb has to work late, and Barb wants to go to the game tonight. The singing of the National Anthem always precedes the game. Carl calls Alice and asks her out to dinner. Due to a thunderstorm, the singing of the National Anthem gets delayed. If Alice goes out to dinner with Carl, she will have to leave work early so she can go home and turn off her crockpot. Alice accepts Carl's invitation. 17.____

CONCLUSION: Barb misses the first inning of the game.

18. FACTS: Earl thinks of any whole number from 1 through 10. Because she is using the most efficient system, Eva absolutely guarantees Earl that she can correctly guess the number he's thinking of in five questions or less. Eva asks Earl a series of *yes/no* questions and guesses the number in five questions or less every time. Earl and Eva agree to play the game again in the exact same way, except that he will think of a whole number from 1 through 6. 18.____

CONCLUSION: Using the same system, four is the absolute highest number of *yes/no* questions that Eva will need to ask in order to guess the number that Earl is thinking of this time.

19. FACTS: Lois will cook dinner today only if Ted, Robbie, and Jennifer are all home by 6 P.M. Robbie will come home by 6 P.M. only if band practice ends early. If Ted plays Softball after work, he will take Jennifer with him, and they will not be home by 6 P.M. Band practice ends early today. 19.____

CONCLUSION: Lois cooks dinner today.

20. FACTS: Three card players each start with $10. Each round they play has two losers and one winner. The losers in each round have to give the winner $2 apiece. Chuck wins the first and third rounds; Bruce wins the second. At the end of the third round, Artie proposes that they change the rules so that the losers each have to give the winner half their accumulated money. They agree, play one more round, and Artie wins it. 20.____

CONCLUSION: At the end of the fourth round, Chuck has less money than Artie.

21. FACTS: No part-time workers at this plant get paid vacations. All cleaners at this plant are part-time workers. Joe gets a paid vacation. 21.____

CONCLUSION: All cleaners at this plant get paid vacations.

22. FACTS: If Myles breaks the lamp, Lucy will scream. If Tom finds Rachel spraying Windex into the cat's dish, he'll scream. If Geoffrey doesn't hear from the French soon, he'll scream. Tom screams. 22.____

CONCLUSION: Myles broke the lamp.

23. FACTS: If Tina goes to the store, Ike will go with her. If Ike goes to the store, he will buy doughnuts. If Dick cleans the house, Sally will go to the store. If Sally goes to the store, Tina will go with her. Dick cleans the house. 23.____

CONCLUSION: Ike buys doughnuts.

24. FACTS: If Joe passes the test, Jill won't apply for the job. If Jill applies for the job, she'll get it. If Jill doesn't apply for the job, Jeanne will be annoyed. Joe passes the test. 24.____

CONCLUSION: Jeanne gets annoyed.

25. FACTS: Mary, Debbie, May, and Joan are the only people waiting for the photocopier to be fixed. When it's fixed, Debbie has to use it first because she's doing work for the boss. Joan has to use it right after the person who's been waiting the longest. The person who has the most work to copy gets to use the machine second. May has been waiting the longest. The person who has been waiting longest is not the person who has the most work to copy. 25.____

CONCLUSION: Joan gets to use the photocopier third.

KEY (CORRECT ANSWERS)

1. B
2. A
3. A
4. C
5. C
6. B
7. B
8. B
9. A
10. C
11. B
12. A
13. A
14. C
15. C
16. C
17. C
18. A
19. C
20. A
21. B
22. C
23. A
24. A
25. B

SOLUTIONS

1. CORRECT ANSWER: B
This is an easy problem if you read it carefully. The third sentence says that Bill types 60 words a minute; the second sentence says that Bill types twice as slow as Charlie. If Bill types twice as slow as Charlie, then Charlie types twice as fast as Bill, or 2 x 60. This means that Charlie types 120 words a minute, not 30 words a minute. These two sentences alone are all you need to disprove the conclusion; the first sentence is just a decoy. If you had *fallen for it* and misread the paragraph, you would most likely have chosen A. You probably would have skimmed the second sentence and assumed that it said *twice as fast*, just because the first sentence said *half as fast.*

2. CORRECT ANSWER: A
This question may look more difficult than it is because the facts are thrown together haphazardly. Many of these logic questions present the *facts* in a very strange fashion. No one would ever talk like this in real life - at least not if they wanted to be understood. The point, of course, is to see how well you can sift through these things, avoid the pitfalls, and find the *truth* of the matter. If you approach a question carefully and attack it systematically, you will usually find that it is not really all that difficult. In this case, by studying the facts, you can see that Albert gets traded. He needs a home run to avoid being traded (sentence 2), but he strikes out in his at-bat (sentence 4). You can assume that this is the at-bat that determines his future because of the way the fourth sentence is worded. It uses the words, *this crucial at-bat.* Knowing the sad truth that he's been traded, you can then trace the chain of events: Chris goes to the Padres (sentence 1), which means that Dave goes to the Dodgers (sentence 3). So the conclusion is, indeed, proved by the facts given to us.

3. CORRECT ANSWER: A
This is a classic form of logic problem, and, like question 2, it doesn't correspond to reality. We all know perfectly well that some beads are cheap, but that has NO bearing on this problem. You often have to let go of your common sense and experience when doing problems like these. Just stick to the facts as they are stated in the problem. The first two sentences are given as facts, and they are enough to prove the conclusion that *all beads are expensive.* In any problem where you are told that a given fact is all-inclusive, such as that *all A are B,* you can just substitute A for B in any other factual sentence in the problem. What is true of B is true of A. Therefore, when you come across another all-inclusive *truth,* such as *all B are C,* you know that *all A are C* must be true too.
Here are two examples. Although only one corresponds to reality as we know it, they both follow the logic formula we've outlined above, and so both are *true* according to logic.

    All dogs (A) are mammals (B).
    All mammals (B) have backbones (C).
    All dogs (A) have backbones (C).

    All apples (A) are bananas (B).
    All bananas (B) have yellow skins (C).
    All apples (A) have yellow skins (C).

Note that this does not work in reverse. All bananas aren't necessarily apples, all things with yellow skins aren't necessarily bananas or apples, and all mammals aren't necessarily dogs. Don't worry if this is confusing to you. The key here is to know the formula and not think about it too much in terms of reality.

In this problem, the *A* is the beads, the *B* is the jewelry, and the *C* is expensive.

4. CORRECT ANSWER: C
This looks a lot like the previous question, but, in fact, the sentences show no relationship between shrimp and shells. You can eliminate the second sentence because it has nothing at all to do with the conclusion. Of the two remaining sentences, one says that mussels have shells, the other says that no shrimp are mussels. This doesn't tell us that no shrimp have shells because it is not really telling us anything about how these two animals compare with each other on this issue. It's as if we said, *all boys like sports* and *no boys are girls.* These statements don't tell us whether girls like sports. They tell us that boys and girls are different, but we don't know how different they are. Are they completely different, or do they have things in common? Is liking sports one of the ways they differ or one of the ways they are alike?

For this reason, there is also nothing in the question to show that shrimp do have shells. Here we have another case where common sense can get you into trouble. You may want to choose answer B, simply because you know that the conclusion is false. But you are not being asked whether the conclusion is true or false; you are being asked whether it is proved true or false by the facts as given. If sentence 3 had said, *only mussels have shells,* then the facts would prove the conclusion, even if that doesn't correspond to reality. But as it is, the facts neither prove nor disprove the conclusion.

5. CORRECT ANSWER: C
This is a tricky one. You may have added all the pounds in the conclusion, and been relieved to find that they totaled the 260 pounds mentioned in the first sentence. You would have been tricked into picking A because the numbers checked out. But it doesn't matter that the numbers match because the problem here is to decide whether the facts prove that those are the exact number of pounds each woman lost. And the facts show that, without knowing Bea's weight loss, we're sure of only one figure - Donna's 80-pound weight loss. This is shown below:

NAME	AMOUNT LOST
Abby	2 x Celia
Bea	?
Celia	1/2 of Abby
Donna	80

You may have tried to work the problem by assuming that Donna's 80 pounds was the highest amount lost because that clue is contained in the problem. If Donna's 80 pounds were the greatest weight loss, Celia would have lost 40 pounds because sentence 3 says that Celia lost half of the greatest amount lost. But this creates a problem because it would mean that Abby also lost 80. Sentence 2 says Abby lost twice what Celia lost. And Abby COULDN'T have lost 80 pounds because that would mean that two women (Abby and Donna) lost the most. This is impossible because sentence 3 says Celia lost half as much as the woman (not <u>women</u>) who lost the most. So the greatest amount lost must have been more than 80 pounds, and Abby must have been the one who lost it. All we know, then, is the following: Donna lost 80 pounds, the greatest amount lost was more than 80 pounds, Celia's amount was half the greatest amount, and Abby lost more than 80 pounds. As long as all these conditions are met, Bea's loss might be any amount that makes up the difference between 260 and the others' total weight loss. For example, the losses could have been:

Abby	84		Abby	90		Abby	94
Bea	54	OR	Bea	45	OR	Bea	39
Celia	42		Celia	45		Celia	47
Donna	<u>80</u>		Donna	<u>80</u>		Donna	<u>80</u>
	260			260			260

Or many other possible combinations. The facts simply don't give us enough information to either prove or disprove that the amounts given in the conclusion are the actual amounts each woman lost. That's why the correct answer is C.

6. CORRECT ANSWER: B
To see why B is the correct answer, it is helpful to draw a diagram of the floors. We know that Ann is on Four (sentence 4) and that Sally is on Three (sentence 3). If Ann is two floors above Brenda (sentence 1), Brenda must be on Two. Now we can draw:

Ann - - - - - - - - - - - - - - (4)
Sally - - - - - - - - - - - - - (3)
Brenda - - - - - - - - - - - (2)

So, if Brenda is one floor below the birthday-girl (sentence 2), today must be Sally's birthday, not Ann's.

7. CORRECT ANSWER: B
Here, you need to know what <u>perpendicular</u> and <u>parallel</u> mean. If you do, a simple diagram should show you that the facts disprove the conclusion. Perpendicular streets are those at right angles to one another, like the two lines in a plus sign (+). Parallel streets are those that run in the same direction, never touching - like the two l's in the word <u>all</u>. The first three facts tell us that the streets look like this:

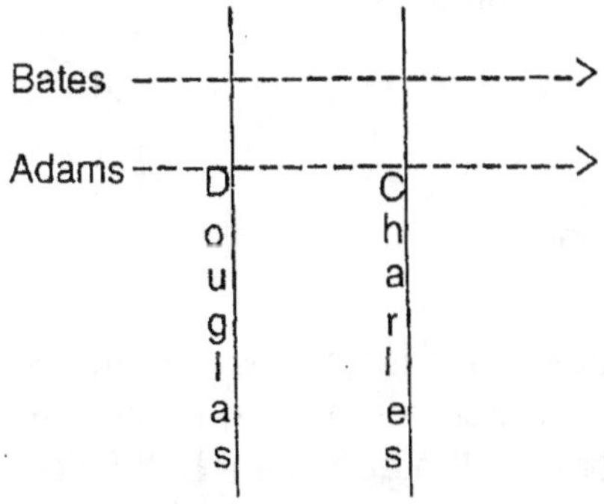

If Evans is parallel to the streets that are perpendicular to Bates (sentence 4), then Evans itself must be perpendicular to Bates. The completed diagram now looks like this:

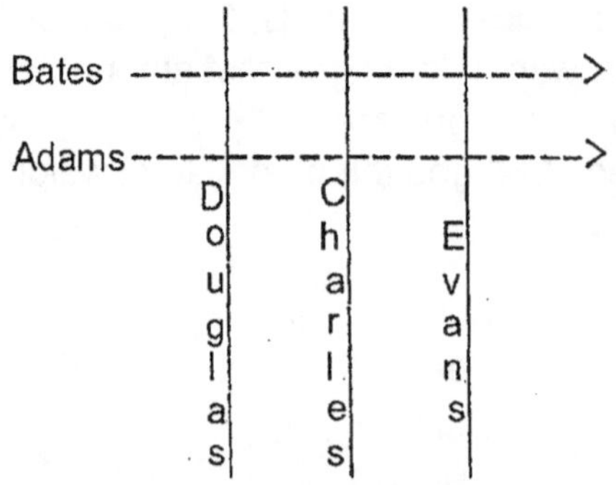

This diagram graphically shows that Evans is NOT perpendicular to Douglas, but parallel to it. The facts, then, disprove the conclusion.

8. CORRECT ANSWER: B
If you start from the last fact given in this problem and work backwards, you will be able to find the cause of each event. This will enable you to either prove or disprove the conclusion. In this case, since the last fact says that the captain ran, that must have been because Arnie hit the ball hard (sentence 3). Even though Arnie hit the ball hard, Bill is out because Bill is so slow that he will be out at home plate (sentence 2). This disproves the conclusion, which says he is safe.

9. CORRECT ANSWER: A
This is an easy problem if you translate the facts into a picture. First of all, ignore sentence 3, which has nothing to do with the problem. Now, draw a circle to represent all the members of this genus (sentence 1). Next, draw a smaller circle to represent the members of that species (sentence 1). You may know that a species is a subgroup of a genus, just as *semi-precious* is a subgroup of gems, or hardwoods is a subgroup of trees. For this reason, the *species* circle should be contained entirely within the *genus* circle. The problem doesn't tell you this about genus and species, but you don't need to know it to answer the question correctly. You could simply place the smaller circle partially in and partially out of the larger circle. No matter which way you portray the relationship, some members of the genus will belong to that species. You can see this in the diagrams below. Since all members of that species are butterflies (sentence 2), the *species* circle also represents butterflies.

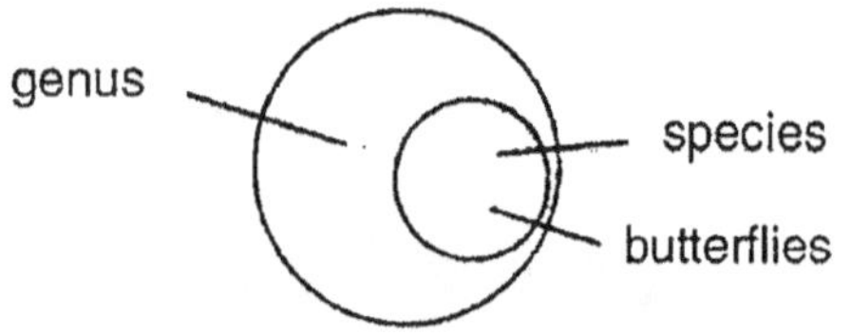

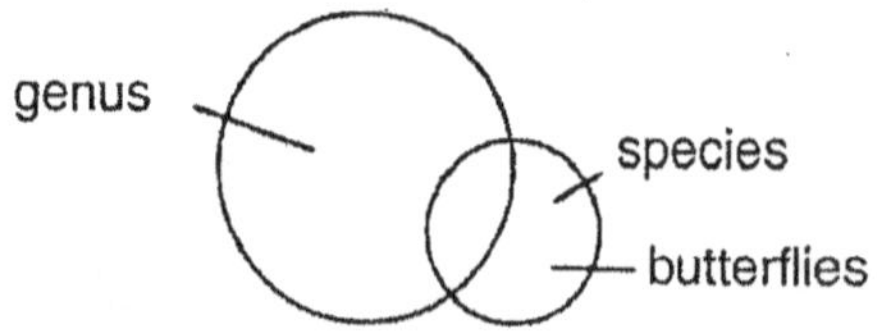

Not <u>all</u> members of this genus are butterflies; this is demonstrated by the fact that there is plenty of room inside the *genus* circle for other, non-butterfly critters. But the picture clearly shows that <u>some</u> members of the genus are butterflies, as the conclusion states.

10. CORRECT ANSWER: C
The facts prove only that some woodwinds (those that are clarinets) are beautiful things; they do not prove that all beautiful things are woodwinds. If you draw circles to represent *beautiful things* and *clarinets,* the latter would have to be a smaller circle inside the former, since all clarinets are beautiful things (sentence 3).

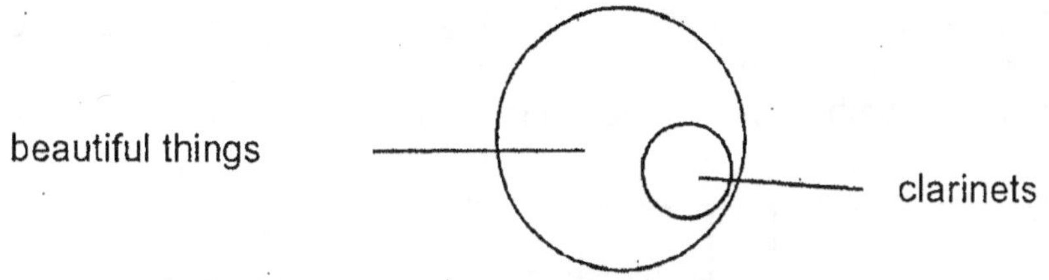

But where does the *woodwind* circle go? All the facts tell us is that some of its members are clarinets. We don't know whether it's bigger, smaller, or the same size as the circle of *beautiful things.* It could look like the following:

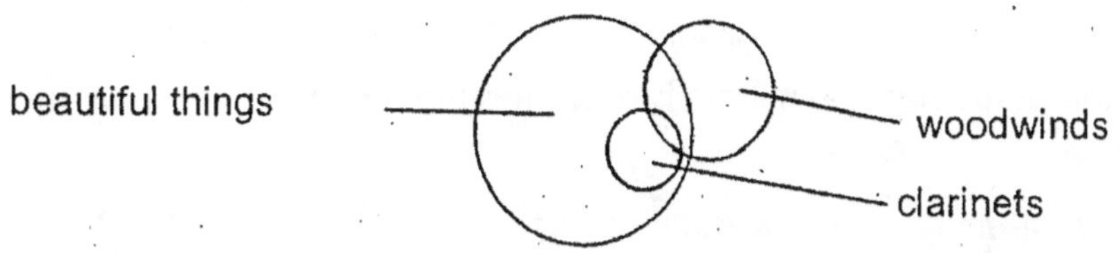

That way, there could be plenty of beautiful things that are not woodwinds, some beautiful things that are woodwinds and clarinets, and some woodwinds that are beautiful things but not clarinets. And the conclusion would be false.
OR, the *woodwinds* circle could be identical to the *beautiful things* circle:

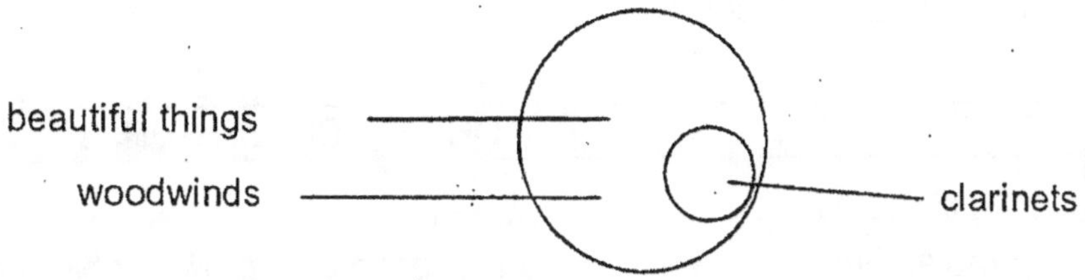

making the conclusion true.
You may have circled answer B, simply because the conclusion is obviously a false statement. But remember, the question is not whether the conclusion is true or false; it's whether it is proved or disproved by the facts given. In this case, it is neither proved nor disproved by the facts. Sentence 2, incidentally, is irrelevant, since the rest of the problem has nothing to do with flutes.

11. CORRECT ANSWER: B
You could use a trial-and-error approach to this problem, but it would be very time-consuming. As you worked with this problem, you may have realized that, since the number in the middle box gets added to every other number, you can solve the problem more easily by putting 6 into the diagram and adding the larger numbers to it to see if it's workable. After placing 6 in the center, you can see there is nowhere to put 9. The horizontal, vertical, and diagonal rows must add up to 15, but wherever you try to put 9, you will have a row that adds up to more than 15. Since 9 + 6 = 15 and 0 is not one of the options, there is no number that can be put in the third box in the row.

	6	
		9

Diagonal

	6	9

Horizontal

	9	
	6	

vertical

So, 6 cannot be the number in the middle box; it's too big. The facts disprove the conclusion.

12. CORRECT ANSWER: A
The first sentence in this problem says that these men bought various colored suits, but not necessarily <u>respectively</u>. This means that the first man (Max) didn't necessarily buy the first color suit (grey), the second man (Nick) didn't necessarily buy the second color suit (green), and so on. <u>Respectively</u> means *in the same order.*
At first glance, this problem looks impossible, but it can be simplified by drawing a chart to show what we *know* about each person:

NAME	PAID	FOR THIS COLOR SUIT
Max	less than Nick	green
Nick	same as Pete	grey (not green, brown or blue)
Pete	same as Nick	blue (not grey, green or brown)
Ollie	2x Nick; 2x Pete	brown

Sentence 2 says Max's suit is green, and sentence 5 says Ollie's is brown, but how do we know Pete's is blue? Well, sentence 4 indicates that someone other than Pete bought the grey one. That means Nick got the grey one. Since the grey, green, and brown suits are all accounted for, the blue one must be Pete's.

Now, all we need to know is who paid the most! Ollie paid twice what Pete paid (sentence 3). This means that he also paid twice what Nick paid because Pete paid the same as the man who bought the grey suit (sentence 4) - and Nick bought the grey suit. So the highest-payer can't be Nick or Pete; it must either be Ollie or Max. But sentence 2 says Max paid <u>less</u> than Nick. So the highest-payer must be Ollie, as proved by the facts given.

13. CORRECT ANSWER: A
The man sitting on Dave's right (sentence 6) has to be Bob because he's the only other man in the group. Alice sits across from Dave (sentence 4). This means that Carol must be sitting across from Bob. From this information, you can draw a diagram of the table and the people seated at it:

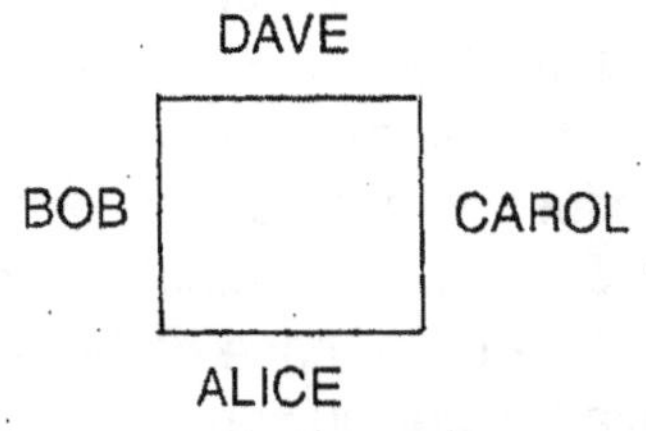

Now all you need to know is whether Dave plays golf. It may help keep everything straight if you put the name of the sport next to the name of the proper person as you figure out each one. Here, we have abbreviated each sport using a lower-case initial (*j* for jogging, *g* for golf, and so on). Since Carol sits to the right of the basketball player (sentence 3), Alice must play basketball. (Remember, it's not Carol's right; it's the basketball player's right. This confuses some people.) Since Bob sits across from the jogger (sentence 2), Carol must jog. After adding this information, your diagram would look like this:

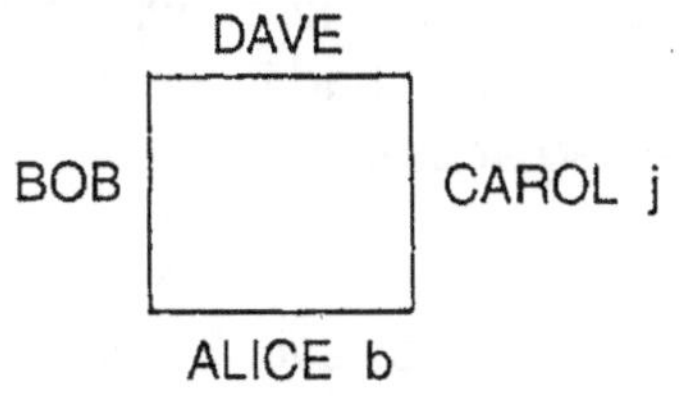

At this point, all you need to know is: Does Bob golf and Dave play tennis, or is it the other way around? A quick trial-and-error produces the answer. Sentence 5 says the golfer sits to the left of the tennis player. If Dave played tennis, would this be true? No. So, it must be Bob who's the tennis player, and Dave who's the golfer. The conclusion is thus proved by the facts. If you have spatial problems, you might want to twist the diagram around to see this more clearly.

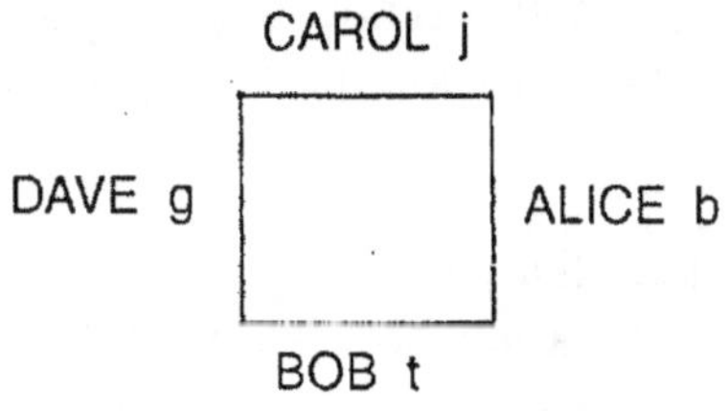

14. CORRECT ANSWER: C
To visualize this problem it is helpful to draw a small chart, showing what we know about each woman's score.

NAME	SCORE
Carol	higher than Betty

Betty	higher than 40 (according to sentence 3 she scored more than twice as high as Alice
Alice	20

From this chart, we can see that Carol's score could have been any number higher than 41. It could have been 50, or 65, or 92–in which case she would have scored high enough to be hired. But it also could have been 42, or 43, or 47–in which case she would not have scored high enough. So, we can't prove that Carol was offered the job, but we can't prove that she wasn't either. In addition, we can't prove that Carol was the only one who was offered the job. We know Alice didn't get an offer (with a score of 20), but we don't know about Betty. She could have gotten anything above 40. So, the facts here neither prove nor disprove the conclusion.

15. CORRECT ANSWER: C
This is a sneaky little question. If you read it quickly, you might have thought it was easy. The cat didn't get rabies (sentence 3), so the cat had had its rabies shots within the last two years (sentence 2). But perhaps the cat didn't get rabies because the squirrel never bit it, or perhaps the squirrel never had rabies to begin with. The first sentence says, *If Camille's squirrel has rabies"* and *(if) the squirrel bites Casey's cat...the cat will get rabies.* (The second *if* is implied by the structure of the sentence.) Nothing in this paragraph ever tells us that the squirrel had rabies or that the squirrel bit the cat. As we said - sneaky. Since you don't know why the cat didn't get rabies, you can't prove that it was spared because it had had its shots, and you can't disprove it either. Therefore, C is the only possible answer.

16. CORRECT ANSWER: C
This is another sneaky question. (The exams haven't used this kind of trick lately, but we wanted to give you practice–just in case.) If you didn't read the problem carefully, you might have chosen B. You would have thought that Laura told Frank (sentence 4), who told Bill (sentence 2), who chose not to fire Sally (sentence 3). Since Sally didn't get fired, she didn't file a grievance (sentence 1). The only problem is that Laura told Fred, not Frank, and we have no way of knowing how Fred fits into this crew. He could have told Frank, thereby setting in motion the cycle above and preventing Sally from getting fired. In that case, the conclusion would be false. Or he could have not told anyone, Sally would have gotten fired, she would have filed a grievance, and the conclusion would have been true. You just don't know, so C is the only option.

17. CORRECT ANSWER: C
Obviously, if the *pre-game* song gets delayed, the game will also be delayed, but we don't know for how long. We also don't know how late Barb had to work. (We know that she did have to work late, because of sentences 1, 5, and 6.) For all we know, the game may have been delayed for an hour due to the storm, and Barb may have had to work only a half hour later than usual–thereby not missing any of the game at all. In questions of this type, it is always good to work backwards from the conclusion and try to see if there is a cause of that conclusion contained in the facts. In this case, although we can find a cause for Barb's having to work late (Alice's acceptance of Carl's invitation), we can find nothing that would necessarily cause Barb to miss the first inning of the game.

18. CORRECT ANSWER: A
The conclusion seems likely because it only takes Eva five tries to guess a number from 1 through 10. The most efficient way to guess is to eliminate half of all possible numbers with each guess. When the number is from 1 through 10, the first question should be, *Is the number you're thinking of 6 or more?* The answer to that question, whether it's yes or no, will eliminate five numbers - half of all the numbers Earl could possibly be thinking of. Let's say Earl said yes. The second question would be, *Is it 8 or more?* That answer will eliminate two or three of the five remaining possible numbers. No matter what range of numbers Earl wants to use, whether it be 1 through 50, 1 through 100, or whatever, Eva could use this method until she narrows the answers down to one possible number. (We can assume that she uses this method because sentence 2 says she is using the most efficient method.)

For the range 1 through 6, then, you can see that four is the highest number of guesses she will need using this system. The most she can be sure of eliminating with one guess is 3 numbers. *(Is the number you're thinking of 4 or more?)* At that point, she may need as many as three more guesses to eliminate the two remaining wrong numbers one by one and then to *guess* the right number. Since this is four guesses, the facts prove the conclusion.

19. CORRECT ANSWER: C
Here is a case in which it is clear that certain facts are missing. You know from sentences 4 and 2 that Robbie is home in time for Lois to make dinner, but what about Ted and Jennifer? Nowhere in the facts does it say whether or not Ted played softball after work. Since sentence 1 says Lois will cook only if all three are home by 6 P.M., we simply don't have enough information to either prove or disprove the conclusion.

20. CORRECT ANSWER: A
Unless you are excellent in math, just about the only way to figure this one out is to set up a grid showing the amount of money each player has after each round. After setting up such a grid, the answer can be found quite easily.

	ARTIE $10	BRUCE $10	CHUCK $10
AFTER ROUND #1	$8	$8	$14
#2	$6	$12	$12
#3	$4	$10	$16
#4	$17	$5	$8

Chuck won the first round (sentence 4). Since everyone started with $10 (sentence 1), you can see that after Round #1, each loser would be out $2 (sentences 2 and 3), bringing their totals down to $8 each. Chuck, on the other hand, would be up to $14, having collected $2 from each of the two losers. The second line of the grid shows the situation after Round #2, which was won by Bruce (sentence 4). The third line shows the situation after Round #3, when Chuck is way ahead (sentence 4). Likewise, the fourth line shows the situation after Round #4, when the rules had been changed and Artie won (sentences 5 and 6). Since each of the other two had to give him half their money (sentence 5), he collected $5 from Bruce and $8 from Chuck. His total of $17 was $9 more than

Chuck had at that point. So, the conclusion that Artie ended up with more money than Chuck is proven by the facts given.

21. CORRECT ANSWER: B
The facts prove just the opposite of the conclusion. If all cleaners work part-time (sentence 2), and no part-timers get paid vacations (sentence 1), then no cleaners can get paid vacations. Where *facts* are given in the form, *No A are B, and all C are A,* you can simply substitute C for A, and that will prove that no C are B. (This is much like question 3, except the first fact is all-exclusive rather than all-inclusive. It excludes rather than includes all of something. See the explanation to question 3, if this is not clear.) In this case, *A* is the part-timers, *B* represents recipients of paid vacations, and *C* is cleaners. The facts disprove the conclusion. Since we don't know what Joe's occupation is, sentence 3 is irrelevant to this problem.

22. CORRECT ANSWER: C
In this case, no amount of *following the trail* of facts will lead you to the conclusion given because there is no trail. No fact implies, or leads to, any other; they are simply a collection of statements with no relationship to one another. The facts neither prove nor disprove the conclusion.

23. CORRECT ANSWER: A
Unlike question 22, this question lends itself to *following the trail* of facts. As we've noticed earlier, a good place to begin the trail is with the last fact. It follows from sentence 5 (Dick cleans the house) that Sally goes to the store (sentence 3), which means that Tina also goes to the store (sentence 4). This, in turn, means that Ike goes (sentence 1), and buys the doughnuts (sentence 2). The facts here prove the conclusion.

24. CORRECT ANSWER: A
To decide whether the facts prove the conclusion, you must understand what each fact means. The fact that Joe passed the test (sentence 4) means that Jill didn't apply for the job (sentence 1). Knowing this, all you have to do is reread sentence 3 to see that Jeanne does, indeed, get annoyed. Sentence 2 is not needed to solve this problem, although it may explain why Jeanne got annoyed.

25. CORRECT ANSWER: B
It is helpful to make a list of who's using the machine when, and to fill in the facts you're given. Then you can gradually deduce more information, until you can see whether the conclusion is proved, disproved, or neither. Sentence 2 says Debbie goes first, so your list, at the start, would look something like this:

First - Debbie
Second - ?
Third - ?
Last - ?

It is clear from sentences 3 and 5 that Joan immediately follows May. This also means that Joan cannot be second, May cannot be last, and Mary cannot be third. You may then wish to enter the possibilities to your list:

First - Debbie
Second - May or Mary

15 (#1)

Third - May or Joan
Last - Joan or Mary

Now, all we need to know is: Does May go second? If so, the conclusion is proved by the facts; if not, it's disproved. We know from sentence 4 that the person with the most work goes second. That person can't be May, however, because May has been waiting longest (sentence 5), and the longest-waiter is not the person with the most work (sentence 6). So, Debbie is first, Mary is second, May is third, Joan is fourth, and the conclusion is disproved.

First - Debbie
Second - Mary
Third - May
Last - Joan

LOGICAL REASONING
EVALUATING CONCLUSIONS IN LIGHT OF KNOWN FACTS

EXAMINATION SECTION

TEST 1

COMMENTARY

This section is designed to provide practice questions in evaluating conclusions when you are given specific data to work with.

We suggest you do the questions three at a time, consulting the answer key and then the solution section for any questions you may have missed. It's a good idea to try the questions again a week before the exam.

In the validity of conclusion type of question, you are first given a reading passage which describes a particular situation. The passage may be on any topic, as it is not your knowledge of the topic that is being tested, but your reasoning abilities. The passage is likely to detail several proposed courses of action and factors affecting these proposals. The reading passage is followed by a conclusion based on the facts in the passage, or a description of a decision taken regarding the situation. The conclusion is followed by a number of statements which have a possible connection to the conclusion. For each statement, you are to determine whether:

A. The statement proves the conclusion.
B. The statement supports the conclusion but does not prove it.
C. The statement disproves the conclusion.
D. The statement weakens the conclusion but does not disprove it.
E. The statement has no relevance to the conclusion.

Remember that the conclusion after the passage is to be accepted as the outcome of what actually happened, and that you are being asked to evaluate the impact each statement would have had on the conclusion.

Questions 1-8.

DIRECTIONS: Questions 1 through 8 are based on the following paragraph.

In May of 2018, Mr. Bryan inherited a clothing store on Main Street in a small New England town. The store has specialized in selling quality men's and women's clothing since 1920. Business has been stable throughout the years, neither increasing nor decreasing. He has an opportunity to buy two adjacent stores which would enable him to add a wider range and style of clothing. In order to do this, he would have to borrow a substantial amount of money. He also risks losing the goodwill of his present clientele.

CONCLUSION: On November 7, 2018, Mr. Bryan tells the owner of the two adjacent stores that he has decided not to purchase them. He feels that it would be best to simply maintain his present marketing position, as there would not be enough new business to support an expansion.

A. The statement proves the conclusion.
B. The statement supports the conclusion but does not prove it.
C. The statement disproves the conclusion.
D. The statement weakens the conclusion.
E. The statement is irrelevant to the conclusion.

1. A large new branch of the county's community college holds its first classes in September. 1.____

2. The town's largest factory shuts down with no indication that it will reopen. 2.____

3. The United States Census showed that the number of children per household dropped from 2.4 to 2.1 since the last census. 3.____

4. Mr. Bryan's brother tells him of a new clothing boutique specializing in casual women's clothing which is opening soon. 4.____

5. Mr. Bryan's sister buys her baby several items for Christmas at Mr. Bryan's store. 5.____

6. Mrs. McIntyre, the President of the Town Council, brings Mr. Bryan a home-baked pumpkin pie in honor of his store's 100th anniversary. They discuss the changes that have taken place in the town, and she comments on how his store has maintained the same look and feel over the years. 6.____

7. In October, Mr. Bryan's aunt lends him $50,000. 7.____

8. The Town Council has just announced that the town is eligible for funding from a federal project designed to encourage the location of new businesses in the central districts of cities and towns. 8.____

Questions 9-18.

DIRECTIONS: Questions 9 through 18 are based on the following paragraph.

A proposal was put before the legislative body of a country to require air bags in all automobiles manufactured for domestic use in that country after 2019. The air bag, made of nylon or plastic, is designed to inflate automatically within a car at the impact of a collision, thus protecting front-seat occupants from being thrown forward. There has been much support of the measure from consumer groups, the insurance industry, key legislators, and the general public. The country's automobile manufacturers, who contend the new crash equipment would add up to $1,000 to car prices and provide no more protection than existing seat belts, are against the proposed legislation

CONCLUSION: On April 21, 2014, the legislation requiring air bags in all automobiles manufactured for domestic use in that country after 2019.

A. The statement proves the conclusion.
B. The statement supports the conclusion but does not prove it.
C. The statement disproves the conclusion.
D. The statement weakens the conclusion.
E. The statement is irrelevant to the conclusion.

9. A study has shown that 59% of car occupants do not use seat belts. 9.____

10. The country's Department of Transportation has estimated that the crash protection equipment would save up to 5,900 lives each year. 10.____

11. On April 27, 2013, Augusta Raneoni was named head of an advisory committee to gather and analyze data on the costs, benefits, and feasibility of the proposed legislation on air bags in automobiles. 11.____

12. Consumer groups and the insurance industry accuse the legislature of rejecting passage of the regulation for political reasons. 12.____

13. A study by the Committee on Imports and Exports projected that the sales of imported cars would rise dramatically in 2019 because imported cars do not have to include air bags, and can be sold more cheaply. 13.____

14. Research has shown that air bags, if produced on a large scale, would cost about $200 apiece, and would provide more reliable protection than any other type of seat belt. 14.____

15. Auto sales in 2011 increased 3% over the previous year. 15.____

16. A Department of Transportation report in July of 2020 credits a drop in automobile deaths of 4,100 to the use of air bags. 16.____

17. In June of 2014, the lobbyist of the largest insurance company receives a bonus for her work on the passage of the air bag legislation. 17.____

18. In 2020, the stock in crash protection equipment has risen three-fold over the previous year. 18.____

Questions 19-25.

DIRECTIONS: Questions 19 through 25 are based on the following paragraph.

On a national television talk show, Joan Rivera, a famous comedienne, has recently insulted the physical appearances of a famous actress and the dead wife of an ex-President. There has been a flurry of controversy over her comments, and much discussion of the incident has appeared in the press. Most of the comments have been negative. It appears that this tie she might have gone too far. There have been cancellations of two of her five scheduled performances in the two weeks since the show was televised, and Joan's been receiving a lot of negative mail. Because of the controversy, she has an interview with a national news magazine at the end of the week, and her press agent is strongly urging her to apologize publicly. She feels strongly that her comments were no worse than any other she has ever made, and that the whole incident will *blow over* soon. She respects her press agent's judgment, however, as his assessment of public sentiment tends to be very accurate.

CONCLUSION: Joan does not apologize publicly, and during the interview she challenges the actress to a weight-losing contest. For every pound the actress loses, Joan says she will donate $1 to the Cellulite Prevention League.

A. The statement proves the conclusion.
B. The statement supports the conclusion but does not prove it.
C. The statement disproves the conclusion.
D. The statement weakens the conclusion.
E. The statement is irrelevant to the conclusion.

19. Joan's mother, who she is very fond of, is very upset with Joan's comments. 19.____

20. Six months after the interview, Joan's income has doubled. 20.____

21. Joan's agent is pleased with the way Joan handles the interview. 21.____

22. Joan's sister has been appointed Treasurer of the Cellulite Prevention League In her report, she states that Joan's $12 contribution is the only amount that has been donated to the League in its first six months. 22.____

23. The magazine receives many letters commending Joan for the courage it took for her to apologize publicly in the interview. 23.____

24. Immediately after the interview appears, another one of Joan's performances is cancelled. 24.____

25. Due to a printers' strike, the article was not published until the following week. 25.____

Questions 26-30.

DIRECTIONS: Questions 25 through 30 are based on the following paragraph.

The law-making body of Country X must decide what to do about the issue of recording television shows for home use. There is currently no law against recording shows directly from the TV as long as the DVDs are not used for commercial purposes. The increasing popularity of pay TV and satellite systems, combined with the increasing number of homes that own recording equipment, has caused a great deal of concern in some segments of the entertainment industry. Companies that own the rights to films, popular television shows, and sporting events feel that their copyright privileges are being violated, and they are seeking compensation or the banning of TV recording. Legislation has been introduced to make it illegal to record television programs for home use. Separate proposed legislation is also pending that would continue to allow recording of TV shows for home use, but would place a tax of 10% on each DVD that is purchased for home use. The income from that tax would then be proportionately distributed as royalties to those owning the rights to programs being aired. A weighted point system coupled with the averaging of several national viewing rating systems would be used to determine the royalties. There is a great deal of lobbying being done for both bills, as the manufacturers of DVDs and recording equipment are against the passage of the bills.

CONCLUSION: The legislature of Country X rejects both bills by a wide margin.

A. The statement proves the conclusion.
B. The statement supports the conclusion but does not prove it.
C. The statement disproves the conclusion.
D. The statement weakens the conclusion.
E. The statement is irrelevant to the conclusion.

26. Country X's Department of Taxation hires 500 new employees to handle the increased paperwork created by the new tax on DVDs. 26.____

27. A study conducted by the country's most prestigious accounting firm shows that the cost of implementing the proposed new DVD tax would be greater than the income expected from it. 27.____

28. It is estimated that 80% of all those working in the entertainment industry, excluding performers, own DVD recorders. 28.____

29. The head of Country X's law enforcement agency states that legislation banning the home recording of TV shows would be unenforceable. 29.____

30. Financial experts predict that unless a tax is placed on DVDs, several large companies in the entertainment industry will have to file for bankruptcy. 30.____

Questions 31-38.

DIRECTIONS: Questions 31 through 38 are variations on the type of question you just had. It is important that you read the question very carefully to determine exactly what is required.

31. In this question, select the choice that is MOST relevant to the conclusion. 31.____
I. The Buffalo Bills football team is in second place in its division.
II. The New England Patriots are in first place in the same division.
III. There are two games left to play in the season, and the Bills will not play the Patriots again.
IV. The New England Patriots won ten games and lost four games, and the Buffalo Bills have won eight games and lost six games.

CONCLUSION: The Buffalo Bills win their division.

A. The conclusion is proved by sentences I-IV.
B. The conclusion is disproved by sentences I-IV.
C. The facts are not sufficient to prove or disprove the conclusion.

32. In this question, select the choice that is MOST relevant to the conclusion. 32.____
I. On the planet of Zeinon there are only two different eye colors and only two different hair colors.
II. Half of those beings with purple hair have golden eyes.
III. There are more inhabitants with purple hair than there are inhabitants with silver hair.
IV. One-third of those with silver hair have green eyes.
CONCLUSION: There are more golden-eyed beings on Zeinon than green-eyed ones.
A. The conclusion is proved by sentences I-IV.
B. The conclusion is disproved by sentences I-IV.
C. The facts are not sufficient to prove or disprove the conclusion.

33. In this question, select the choice that is MOST relevant to the conclusion. 33.____
John and Kevin are leaving Amaranth to go to school in Bethany. They've decided to rent a small truck to move their possessions. Joe's Truck Rental charges $100 plus 30¢ a mile. National Movers charges $50 more but gives free mileage for the first 100 miles. After the first 100 miles, they charge 25¢ a mile.
CONCLUSION: John and Kevin rent their truck from National Movers because it is cheaper.
A. The conclusion is proved by the facts in the above paragraph.
B. The conclusion is disproved by the facts in the above paragraph.
C. The facts are not sufficient to prove or disprove the conclusion.

34. For this question, select the choice that supports the information given in the passage. 34.____
Municipalities in Country X are divided into villages, towns, and cities. A village has a population of 5,000 or less. The population of a town ranges from 5,001 to 15,000. In order to be incorporated as a city, the municipality must have a population over 15,000. If, after a village becomes a town, or a town becomes a city, the population drops below the minimum required (for example, the population of a city goes below 15,000), and stays below the minimum for more than ten years, it loses its current status, and drops to the next category. As soon as a municipality rises in population to the next category (village to town, for example), however, it is immediately reclassified to the next category.
In the 2000 census, Plainfield had a population of 12,000. Between 2000 and 2010, Plainfield grew 10%, and between 2010 and 2020 Plainfield grew another 20%. The population of Springdale doubled from 2000 to 2010, and increased 25% from 2010 to 2020. The city of Smallville's population, 20,283, has not changed significantly in recent years. Granton had a population of 25,000 people in1990, and has decreased 25% in each ten year period since then. Ellenville had a population of 4,283 in 1990, and grew 5% in each ten year period since 1990.

In 2020,

A. Plainfield, Smallville, and Granton are cities.
B. Smallville is a city, Granton is a town, and Ellenville is a village.
C. Springdale, Granton, and Ellenville are towns.
D. Plainfield and Smallville are cities, and Ellenville is a town.

35. For this question, select the choice that is MOST relevant to the conclusion. 35.____

A study was done for a major food-distributing firm to determine if there is any difference in the kind of caffeine containing products used by people of different ages. A sample of one thousand people between the ages of twenty and fifty were drawn from selected areas in the country. They were divided equally into three groups.

Those individuals who were 20-29 were designated Group A, those 30-39 were Group B, and those 40-50 were placed in Group C.

It was found that on the average, Group A drank 1.8 cups of coffee, Group B 3.1, and Group C 2.5 cups of coffee daily. Group A drank 2.1 cups of tea, Group B drank 1.2, and Group C drank 2.6 cups of tea daily. Group A drank 3 1.8 ounces glasses of cola, Group B drank 1.9, and Group C drank 1.5 glasses of cola daily.

CONCLUSION: According to the study, the average person in the 20-29 age group drinks less tea daily than the average person in the 40-50 age group, but drinks more coffee daily than the average person in the 30-39 age group drinks cola.

A. The conclusion is proved by the facts in the above paragraph.
B. The conclusion is disproved by the facts in the above paragraph.
C. The facts are not sufficient to prove or disprove the conclusion.

36. For this question, select the choice that is MOST relevant to the conclusion 36.____

I. Mary is taller than Jane but shorter than Dale.
II. Fred is taller than Mary but shorter than Steven.
III. Dale is shorter than Steven but taller than Elizabeth.
IV. Elizabeth is taller than Mary but not as tall as Fred.

CONCLUSION: Dale is taller than Fred.

A. The conclusion is proved by sentences I-IV.
B. The conclusion is disproved by sentences I-IV.
C. The facts are not sufficient to prove or disprove the conclusion.

37. For this question, select the choice that is MOST relevant to the conclusion. 37.____

I. Main Street is between Spring Street and Glenn Blvd.
II. Hawley Avenue is one block south of Spring Street and three blocks north of Main Street.
III. Glenn Street is five blocks south of Elm and four blocks south of Main.
IV. All the streets mentioned are parallel to one another.

CONCLUSION: Elm Street is between Hawley Avenue and Glenn Blvd.

A. The conclusion is proved by the facts in sentences I-IV.
B. The conclusion is disproved by the facts in sentences I-IV.
C. The facts are not sufficient to prove or disprove the conclusion.

38. For this question, select the choice that is MOST relevant to the conclusion. 38.____
   I. Train A leaves the town of Hampshire every day at 5:50 A.M. and arrives in New London at 6:42 A.M.
   II. Train A leaves New London at 7:00 A.M. and arrives in Kellogsville at 8:42 A.M.
   III. Train B leaves Kellogsville at 8:00 A.M. and arrives in Hampshire at 10:45 A.M.
   IV. Due to the need for repairs, there is just one railroad track between New London and Hampshire.

   CONCLUSION: It is impossible for Train A and Train B to follow these schedules without colliding.

   A. The conclusion is proved by the facts in sentences I-IV.
   B. The conclusion is disproved by the facts in sentences I-IV.
   C. The facts are not sufficient to prove or disprove the conclusion.

KEY (CORRECT ANSWERS)

1.	D	11.	C	21.	D	31.	C
2.	B	12.	C	22.	A	32.	A
3.	E	13.	D	23.	C	33.	C
4.	B	14.	B	24.	B	34.	B
5.	C	15.	E	25.	E	35.	B
6.	A	16.	B	26.	C	36.	C
7.	D	17.	A	27.	B	37.	A
8.	B	18.	B	28.	E	38.	B
9.	B	19.	D	29.	B		
10.	B	20.	E	30.	D		

SOLUTIONS TO QUESTIONS

1. The answer is D. This statement weakens the conclusion, but does not disprove it. If a new branch of the community college opened in September, it could possibly bring in new business for Mr. Bryant. Since it states in the conclusion that Mr. Bryant felt there would not be enough new business to support the additional stores, this would tend to disprove the conclusion. Choice C would not be correct because it's possible that he felt that the students would not have enough additional money to support his new venture, or would not be interested in his clothing styles. It's also possible that the majority of the students already live in the area, so that they wouldn't really be a new customer population. This type of question is tricky, and can initially be very confusing, so don't feel badly if you missed it. Most people need to practice with a few of these types of questions before they feel comfortable recognizing exactly what they're being asked to do.

2. The answer is B. It supports the conclusion because the closing of the factory would probably take money and customers out of the town, causing Mr. Bryant to lose some of his present business. It doesn't prove the conclusion, however, because we don't know how large the factory was. It's possible that only a small percentage of the population was employed there, or that they found other jobs.

3. The answer is E. The fact that the number of children per household dropped slightly nationwide in the decade is irrelevant. Statistics showing a drop nationwide doesn't mean that there was a drop in the number of children per household in Mr. Bryant's hometown. This is a tricky question, as choice B, supporting the conclusion but not proving it, may seem reasonable. If the number of children per household declined nationwide, then it may not seem unreasonable to feel that this would support Mr. Bryant's decision not to expand his business. However, we're preparing you for promotional exams, not "real life." One of the difficult things about taking exams is that sometimes you're forced to make a choice between two statements that both seem like they could be the possible answer. What you need to do in that case is choose the best choice. Becoming annoyed or frustrated with the question won't really help much. If there's a review of the exam, you can certainly appeal the question. There have been many cases where, after an appeal, two possible choices have been allowed as correct answers. We've included this question, however, to help you see what to do should you get a question like this. It's most important not to get rattled, and to select the BEST choice. In this case, the connection between the statistical information and Mr. Bryant's decision is pretty remote. If the question had said that the number of children in Mr. Bryant's <u>town</u> had decreased, then choice B would have been a more reasonable choice. It could also help in this situation to visualize the situation. Picture Mr. Bryant in his armchair reading that, nationwide, the average number of children per household has declined slightly. How likely would this be to influence his decision, especially since he sells men's and women's clothing? It would take a while for this decline in population to show up, and we're not even sure if it applies to Mr. Bryant's hometown. Don't feel badly if you missed this; it was tricky. The more of these you do, the more comfortable you'll feel.

4. The answer is B. If a new clothing boutique specializing in casual women's clothing were to open soon, this would lend support to Mr. Bryant's decision not to expand, but would not prove that he had actually made the decision to expand. A new women's clothing boutique would most likely be in competition with his existing business, thus making any possible expansion a riskier venture. We can't be sure from this, however, that he didn't go ahead and expand his business despite the increased competition. Choice A, proves the conclusion, would only be the answer if we could be absolutely sure from the statement that Mr. Bryant had actually <u>not</u> expanded his business.

5. The answer is C. This statement disproves the conclusion. In order for his sister to buy several items for her baby at Mr. Bryant's store, he would have to have changed his business to include children's clothing.

6. The answer is A. It definitely proves the conclusion. The passage states that Mr. Bryan's store had been in business since 1920. A pie baked in honor of his store's 100th anniversary would have to be presented sometime in 2020. The conclusion states that he made his decision not to expand on November 7, 2018. If, more than a year later Mrs. MacIntyre comments that his store has maintained the same look and feel over the years, it could not have been expanded, or otherwise significantly changed.

7. The answer is D. If Mr. Bryant's aunt lent him $50,000 in October, this would tend to weaken the conclusion, which took place in November. Because it was stated that Mr. Bryant would need to borrow money in order to expand his business, it would be logical to assume that if he borrowed money he had decided to expand his business, weakening the conclusion. The reason C, disproves the conclusion, is not the correct answer is because we can't be sure Mr. Bryant didn't borrow the money for another reason.

8. The answer is B. If Mr. Bryant's town is eligible for federal funds to encourage the location of new businesses in the central district, this would tend to support his decision not to expand his business. Funds to encourage new business would increase the likelihood of there being additional competition for Mr. Bryant's store to contend with. Since we can't say for sure that there would be direct competition from a new business, however, choice A would be incorrect. Note that this is also a tricky question. You might have thought that the new funds weakened the conclusion because it would mean that Mr. Bryant could easily get the money he needed. Mr. Bryant is expanding his present business, not creating a <u>new</u> business. Therefore, he is not eligible for the funding.

9. The answer is B. This is a very tricky question. It's stated that 59% of car occupants don't use seat belts. The legislature is considering the use of air bags because of safety issues. The advantage of air bags over seat belts is that they inflate upon impact, and don't require car occupants to do anything with them ahead of time. Since the population has strongly resisted using seat belts, the air bags could become even more important in saving lives. Since saving lives is the purpose of the proposed legislation, the information that a small percentage of people use seat belts could be helpful to the passage of the legislation. We can't be sure that this is reason enough for the legislature to vote for the legislation, however, so choice A in incorrect.

10. The answer is B, as the information that 5,900 lives could be saved would tend to support the conclusion. Saving that many lives through the use of air bags could be a very persuasive reason to vote for the legislation. Since we don't know for sure that it's enough of a compelling reason for the legislature to vote for the legislation, however, choice A could not be the answer.

11. The answer is C, disproves the conclusion. If the legislation had been passed as stated in the conclusion, there would be no reason to appoint someone head of an advisory committee six days later to analyze the "feasibility of the proposed legislation." The key word here is "proposed." If it has been proposed, it means it hasn't been passed. This contradicts the conclusion and, therefore, disproves it.

12. The answer is C, disproves the conclusion. If the legislation had passed, there would be no reason for supporters of the legislation to accuse the legislature of rejecting the legislation for political reasons. This question may have seemed so obvious that you might have thought there was a trick to it. Exams usually have a few obvious questions, which will trip you up if you begin reading too much into them.

13. The answer is D, as this would tend to disprove the conclusion. A projected dramatic rise in imported cars could be very harmful to the country's economy and could be a very good reason for some legislators to vote against the proposed legislation. It would be assuming too much to choose C, however, because we don't know if they actually did vote against it.

14. The answer is B. This information would tend to support the passage of the legislation. The estimate of the cost of the air bags is $800 less than the cost estimated by opponents, and it's stated that the protection would be more reliable than any other type of seat belt. Both of these would be good arguments in favor of passing the legislation. Since we don't know for sure, however, how persuasive they actually were, choice A would not be the correct choice.

15. The answer is E, as this is irrelevant information. It really doesn't matter whether auto sales in 2001 have increased slightly over the previous year. If the air bag legislation were to go into effect in 2004, that might make the information somehow more relevant. But the air bag legislation would not take effect until 2009, so the information is irrelevant, since it tells us nothing about the state of the auto industry then.

16. The answer is B, supports the conclusion. This is a tricky question. While at first it might seem to prove the conclusion, we can't be sure that the air bag legislation is responsible for the drop in automobile deaths. It's possible air bags came into popular use without the legislation, or with different legislation. There's no way we can be sure that it was the proposed legislation mandating the use of air bags that was responsible.

17. The answer is A. If, in June of 2009, the lobbyist received a bonus "for her work on the air bag legislation," we can be sure that the legislation passed. This proves the conclusion.

18. The answer is B. This is another tricky question. A three-fold stock increase would strongly suggest that the legislation had been passed, but it's possible that factors other than the air bag legislation caused the increase. Note that the stock is in "crash protection

equipment." Nowhere in the statement does it say air bags. Seat belts, motorcycle helmets, and collapsible bumpers are all crash protection equipment and could have contributed to the increase. This is just another reminder to read carefully because the questions are often designed to mislead you.

19. The answer is D. This would tend to weaken the conclusion because Joan is very fond of her mother and she would not want to upset her unnecessarily. It does not prove it, however, because if Joan strongly feels she is right, she probably wouldn't let her mother's opinion sway her. Choice E would also not be correct, because we cannot assume that Joan's mother's opinion is of so little importance to her as to be considered irrelevant.

20. The answer is E. The statement is irrelevant. We are told that Joan's income has doubled but we are not old why. The phrase "six months after the interview" can be misleading in that it leads us to assume that the increase and the interview are related. Her income could have doubled because she regained her popularity but it could also have come from stocks or some other business venture. Because we are not given any reason for her income doubling, it would be impossible to say whether or not this statement proves or disproves the conclusion. Choice E is the best choice of the five possible choices. One of the problems with promotional exams is that sometimes you need to select a choice you're not crazy about. In this case, "not having enough information to made a determination" would be the best choice. However, that's not an option, so you're forced to work with what you've got. On these exams it's sometimes like voting for President; you have to pick the "lesser of the two evils" or the least awful choice. In this case, the information is more irrelevant to the conclusion than it is anything else.

21. The answer is D, weakens the conclusion. We've been told that Joan's agent feels that she should apologize. If he is pleased with her interview, then it would tend to weaken the conclusion but not disprove it. We can't be sure that he hasn't had a change of heart, or that there weren't other parts of the interview he liked so much that they outweighed her unwillingness to apologize.

22. The answer is A. The conclusion states that Joan will donate $1 to the Cellulite Prevention League for every pound the actress loses. Joan's sister's financial report on the League's activities directly supports and proves the conclusion.

23. The answer is C, disproves the conclusion. If the magazine receives many letters commending Joan for her courage in apologizing, this directly contradicts the conclusion, which states that Joan didn't apologize.

24. The answer is B. It was stated in the passage that two of Joan's performances were cancelled after the controversy first occurred. The cancellation of another performance immediately after her interview was published would tend to support the conclusion that she refused to apologize. Because we can't be sure, however, that her performance wasn't cancelled for another reason, choice A would be incorrect.

25. The answer is E, as this information is irrelevant. Postponing the article an extra week does not affect Joan's decision or the public's reaction to it.

26. The answer is C. If 500 new employees are hired to handle the "increased paperwork created by the new tax on DVDs," this would directly contradict the conclusion, which states that the legislature defeated both bills. (They should all be this easy.)

27. The answer is B. The results of the study would support the conclusion. If implementing the legislation was going to be so costly, it is likely that the legislature would vote against it. Choice A is not the answer, however, because we can't be sure that the legislature didn't pass it anyway.

28. The answer is E. It's irrelevant to the conclusion that 80% of all those working in the entertainment industry own DVD recorders. Sometimes if you're not sure about these, it can help a lot to try and visualize the situation. Why would someone voting on this legislation care about this fact? It doesn't seem to be the kind of information that would make any difference or impact upon the conclusion.

29. The answer is B. The head of the law enforcement agency's statement that the legislation would be unenforceable would support the conclusion. It's possible that many legislators would question why they should bother to pass legislation that would be impossible to enforce. Choice A would be incorrect, however, because we can't be sure that the legislation wasn't passed in spite of his statement.

30. The answer is D. This would tend to weaken the conclusion because the prospect of several large companies going bankrupt would seem to be a good argument in favor of the legislation. The possible loss of jobs and businesses would be a good reason for some people to vote for the legislation. We can't be sure, however, that this would be a competing enough reason to ensure passage of the legislation so choice C is incorrect.

This concludes our section on the "Validity of Conclusion" type of questions. We hope these weren't too horrible for you. It's important to keep in mind <u>exactly</u> what you've been given and <u>exactly</u> what they want you to do with it. It's also necessary to remember that you may have to choose between two possible answers. In that case, you must choose the one that seems the best. Sometimes you may think there is no good answer. You will probably be right, but you can't let that upset you. Just choose the one you dislike the least.

We want to repeat that it is unlikely that this exact format will appear on the exam. The skills required to answer these questions, however, are the same as those you'll need for the exam so we suggest that you review this section before taking the actual exam.

31. The answer is C. This next set of questions requires you to "switch gears" slightly, and get used to different formats. In this type of question, you have to decide whether the conclusion is proved by the facts give, disproved by the facts given, or neither because note enough information has been provided. Fortunately, unlike the previous questions, you don't have to decide whether particular facts support or don't support the conclusion. This type of question is more straight forward, but the reasoning behind it is the same. We are told that the Bills have won two games less than the Patriots, and that the Patriots are in first place and the Bills are in second place. We are also told that there are two games left to play, and that they won't play each other again. The conclusion states that the Bills won the division. Is there anything in the four statements that would prove this? We have

no idea what the outcome of the last two games of the season was. The Bills and Patriots could have ended up tied at the end of the season, or the Bills could have lost both or one of their last games while the Patriots did the same. There might even be another team tied for first or second place with the Bills or Patriots. Since we don't know for sure, Choice A is incorrect. Choice B is trickier. It might seem at first glance that the best the Bills could do would be to tie the Patriots if the Patriots lost their last two games and the Bills won their last two games. But it would be too much to assume that there is no procedure for a tiebreaker that wouldn't give the Bills the division championship. Since we don't know what the rules are in the event of a tie (for example, what if a tie was decided on the results of what happened when the two teams had played each other, or on the best record in the division, or on most points scored?), we can't say for sure that it would be impossible for the Bills to win their division. For this reason, choice C is the answer, as we don't have enough information to prove or disprove the conclusion. This question looked more difficult than it actually was. It's important to disregard any factors outside of the actual question, and to focus only on what you've been given. In this case, as on all of these types of questions, what you know or don't know about a subject is actually irrelevant. It's best to concentrate only on the actual facts given.

32. The answer is A. The conclusion is proved by the facts given.

In this type of problem, it is usually best to pull as many facts as possible from the sentences and then put them into a simpler form. The phrasing and the order of exam questions are designed to be confusing so you need to restate things as clearly as possible by eliminating the extras.

Sentence I tells us that there are only two possible colors for eyes and two for hair. Looking at the other sentences we learn that eyes are either green or gold and that hair is either silver or purple. If half the beings with purple hair have golden eyes, then the other half must have green eyes since it is the only other eye color. Likewise, if one-third of those with silver hair have green eyes, the other two-thirds must have golden eyes.

This information makes it clear that there are more golden-eyed beings on Zeinon than green-eyed ones. It doesn't matter that we don't know exactly how many are actually living on the planet. The number of those with gold eyes (1/2 plus 2/3) will always be greater than the number of those with green eyes (1/2 plus 1/3), no matter what the actual figures might be. Sentence III is totally irrelevant because even if there were more silver-haired inhabitants it would not affect the conclusion.

33. The answer is C. The conclusion is neither proved nor disproved by the facts because we don't know how many miles Bethany is from Amoranth.

With this type of question, if you're not sure how to approach it, you can always substitute in a range of "real numbers" to see what the result would be. If they were 200 miles apart, Joe's Truck Rental would be cheaper because they would charge a total of $160 while National Movers would charge $175.

Joe's - $100 plus .30 x 200 (or $60) = $160
National - $150 plus .25 x 100 (or $25) = $175

If the towns were 600 miles apart, however, National Movers would be cheaper. The cost of renting from National would be $275 compared to the $280 charged by Joe's Trucking.

Joe's - $100 plus .30 x 600 (or $180) = $280
National - $150 plus .25 x 500 (or $125) = $275

34. The answer is B. We've varied the format once more, but the reasoning is similar. This is a tedious question that is more like a math question, but we wanted to give you some practice with this type, just in case. You won't be able to do this question if you've forgotten how to do percents. Many exams require this knowledge, so if you feel you need a review we suggest you read Booklets 1, 2 or 3 in this series.

The only way to attack this problem is to go through each choice until you find the one that is correct. Choice A states that Plainfield, Smallville, and Granton are cities. Let's begin with Plainfield. The passage states that in 1990 Plainfield had a population of 12,000, and that it grew 10% between 1990 and 2000, and another 20% between 2000 and 2010. Ten percent of 12,000 is 1200 (12,000 x .10 = 1200). Therefore, the population grew from 12,000 in 1990 to 12,000 + 1200 between 1990 and 2000. At the time of the 2000 Census, Plainfield's population was 13,200. It then grew another 20% between 2000 and 2010, so, 13,200 x .20 = 2640. 13,200 plus the additional increase of 2640 would make the population of Plainfield 15,840. This would qualify it as a city, since its population is over 15,000. Since a change upward in the population of a municipality is re-classified immediately, Plainfield would have become a city right away. So far, statement A is true. The passage states that Smallville's population has not changed significantly in the last twenty years. Since Smallville's population was 20,283, Smallville would still be a city. Granton had a population of 25,000 (what a coincidence that so any of these places have such nice, even numbers) in 1980. The population has decreased 25% in each ten year period since that time. So from 1980 to 1990, the population decreased 25%. 25,000 x .25 = 6,250. 25,000 minus 6,250 = 18,750. So the population of Granton in 1990 would have been 18,750. (Or, you could have saved a step and multiplied 25,000 by .75 to get 18,750.) The population from 1990 to 2000 decreased an additional 25%. So: 18,750 x .25 = 4,687.50. 18,750 minus 4,687.50 = 14,062.50. Or: 18,750 x .75 = 14,062.50. (Don't let the fact that a half of a person is involved confuse you; these are exam questions, not real life.) From 2000 to 2010 the population decreased an additional 25%. This would mean that Granton's population was below 15,000 for more than ten years, so it's status as a city would have changed to that of a town, which would make choice A incorrect.

Choice B states that Smallville is a city and Granton is a town, which we know to be true from the information above. Choice B is correct so far. We next need to determine if Ellenville is a village. Ellenville had a population of 4,283 in 1980, and increased 5% in each ten year period since 1980. 4,283 x .05 = 214.15. 4,283 plus 214.15 = 4,497.15, so Ellenville's population from 1980 to 1990 increased to 4,497.15. (Or: 4,283 x 1.05 – 4,497.15.) From 1990 to 2000 Ellenville's population increased another 5%: 4,497.15 x .05 = 224.86. 4,497.15 plus 224.86 = 4,772.01 (or: 4,497.15 x 1.05 = 4,722.01.) From 2000 to 2010, Ellenville's population increased another 5%: 4,722.01 x .05 = 236.10. 4,722.01 plus 236.10 = 4,958.11. (Or: 4,722.01 x 1.05 = 4,958.11.).

Ellenville's population is still under 5,000 in 2010, so it would continue to be classified as a village. Since all three statements in choice B are true, choice B must be the answer. However, we'll go through the other choices. Choice C states that Springdale is a town. The passage tells us that the population of Springdale doubled from 1990 to 2000, and increased 25% from 2000 to 2010. It doesn't give us any actual population figures, however, so it's impossible to know what the population of Springdale is, making choice C incorrect. Choice C also states that Granton is a town, which is true, and that Ellenville is a town, which is false (from choice B we know it's a village). Choice D states that Plainfield and Smallville are cities, which is information we already know is true, and that Ellenville is a town. Since Ellenville is a village, choice D is also incorrect.

This was a lot of work for just one question and we doubt you'll get one like this on this section of the exam, but we included it just in case. On an exam, you can always put a check mark next to a question like this and come back to it later, if you feel you're pressed for time and cold spend your time more productively on other, less time-consuming problems.

35. The answer is B. This question requires very careful reading. It's best to break the conclusion down into smaller parts in order to solve the problem. The first half of the conclusion states that the average person in the 20-29 age group (Group A) drinks less tea daily than the average person in the 40-50 age group (Group C). The average person in Group A drinks 2.1 cups of tea daily, while the average person in Group C drinks 2.6 cups of tea daily. Since 2.1 is less than 2.6, the conclusion is correct so far. The second half of the conclusion states that the average person in Group A drinks more coffee daily than the average person in the 30-39 age group (Group B) drinks cola. The average person in Group A drinks 1.8 cups of coffee daily, while the average person in Group B drinks 1.9 glasses of cola. This disproves the conclusion, which states that the average person in Group A drinks more coffee daily than the average person in Group B drinks cola.

36. The answer is C. The easiest way to approach a problem that deals with the relationship between a number of different people or things is to set up a diagram. This type of problem is usually too confusing to do in your head. For this particular problem, the "diagram" could be a line, one end of which would be labeled tall and the other end labeled short. Then, taking one sentence at a time, place the people on the line to see where they fall in relation to one another.

The diagram of the first sentence would look like this:

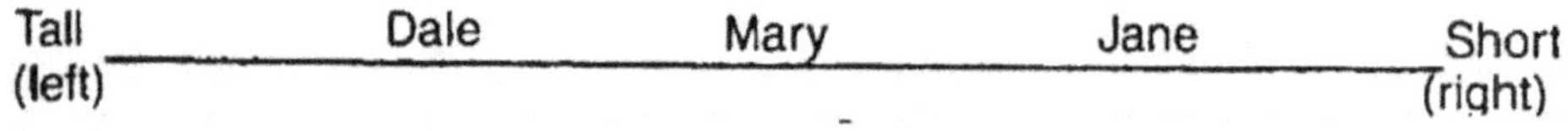

Mary is taller than Jane but shorter than Dale, so she would fall somewhere between the two of them. We have placed tall on the left and labeled it left just to make the explanation easier. You could just as easily have reversed the position.

The second sentence places Fred somewhere to the left of Mary because he is taller than she is. Steven would be to the left of Fred for the same reason. At this point we don't know whether Steven and Fred are taller or shorter than Dale. The new diagram would look like this:

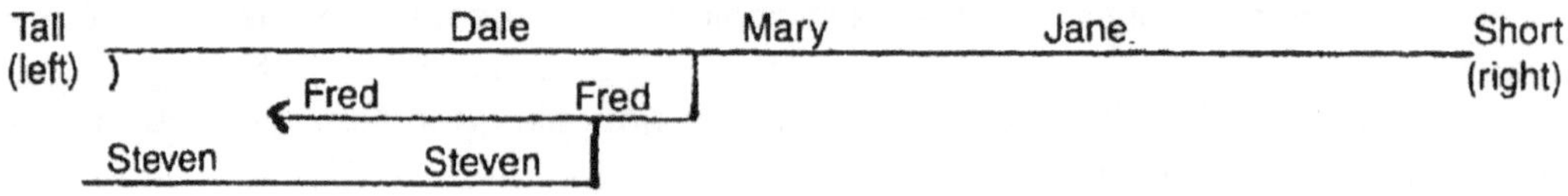

The third sentence introduces Elizabeth, presenting a new problem. Elizabeth can be anywhere to the right of Dale. Don't make the mistake of assuming she falls between Dale and Mary. At this point we don't know where she fits in relation to Mary, Jane, or even Fred.

We do get information about Steven, however. He is taller than Dale so he would be to the left of Dale. Since he is also taller than Fred (see sentence II), we know that Steven is the tallest person thus far. The diagram would now look like this:

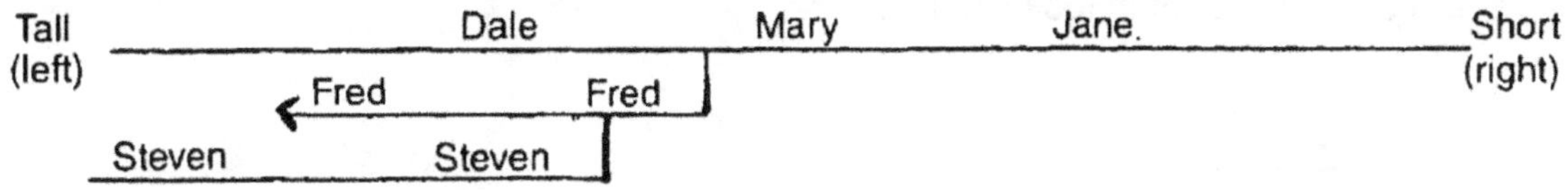

Fred's height is somewhere between Steven and Mary, Elizabeth's anywhere between Dale and the end of the line.

The fourth sentence tells us where Elizabeth stands, in relation to Fred and the others in the problem. The fact that she is taller than Mary means she is also taller than Jane. The final diagram would look like this:

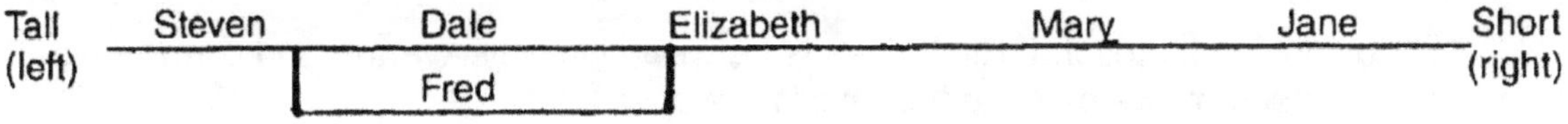

We still don't know whether Dale or Fred is taller, however. Therefore, the conclusion that Dale is taller than Fred can't be proved. It also can't be disproved because we don't know for sure that he isn't. The answer has to be choice C, as the conclusion can't be proved or disproved.

37. The answer is A. This is another problem that is easiest for most people if they make a diagram. Sentence I states that Main Street is between Spring Street and Glenn Blvd. At this point we don't know if they are next to each other or if they are separated by a number of streets. Therefore, you should leave space between streets as you plot your first diagram.

The order of the streets could go either:

Spring St. Main St. Glenn Blvd.	or	Glenn Blvd. Main St. Spring St.

Sentence II states that Hawley Street is one block south of Spring Street and 3 blocks north of Main Street. Because most people think in terms of north as above and south as below and because it was stated that Hawley is one block south of Spring Street and three blocks north of Main Street, the next diagram could look like this:

Spring
Hawley
______
______
Main
Glenn

The third sentence states that Glenn Street is five blocks south of Elm and four blocks south of Main. It could look like this:

Spring
Hawley
______
Elm
Main
____
____
____
Glenn

The conclusion states that Elm Street is between Hawley Avenue and Glenn Blvd. From the above diagram, we can see that this is the case.

38. The answer is B. For most people, the best way to do this problem is to draw a diagram, plotting the course of both trains. Sentence I states that Train A leaves Hampshire at 5:50 A.M. and reaches New London at 6:42. Your first diagram might look like this:

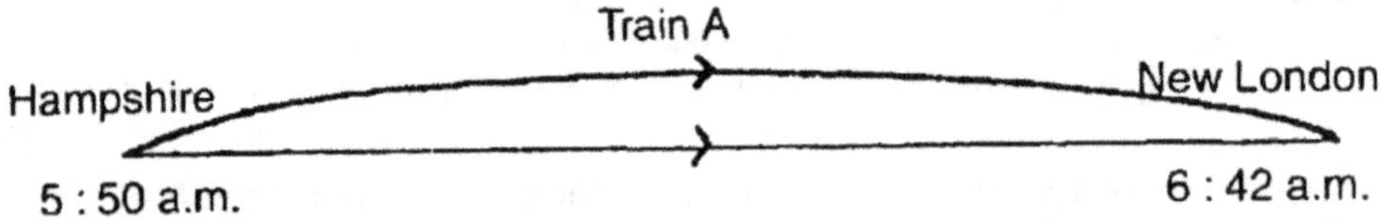

Sentence II states that the train leaves New London at 7:00 a.m. and arrives in Kellogsville at 8:42 a.m. The diagram might now look like this:

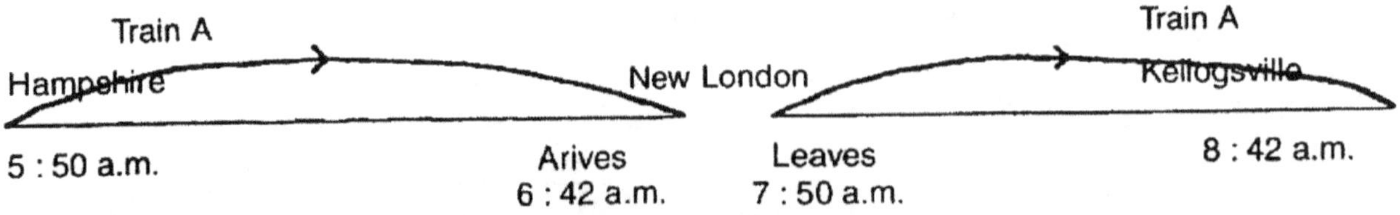

Sentence III gives us the rest of the information that must be included in the diagram. It introduces Train B, which moves in the opposite direction, leaving Kellogsville at 8:00 a.m. and arriving at Hampshire at 10:42 a.m. The final diagram might look like this:

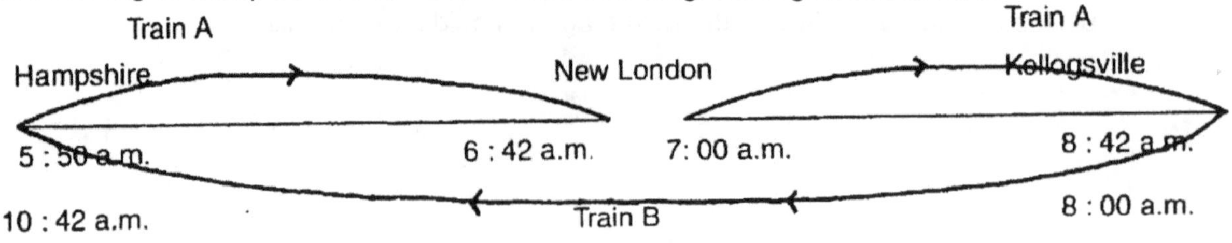

19 (#1)

As you can see from the diagram, the routes of the two trains will overlap somewhere between Kellogsville and New London. If you read sentence IV quickly and assumed that that was the section with only one track, you probably would have assumed that there would have had to be a collision. Sentence IV states, however, that there is only one railroad track between New London and Hampshire. That is the only section, then, where the two trains could collide. By the time Train B gets to that section, however, Train A will have passed it. The two trains will pass each other somewhere between New London and Kellogsville, not New London and Hampshire.

EXAMINATION SECTION

TEST 1

DIRECTIONS: Each question or incomplete statement is followed by several suggested answers or completions. Select the one that BEST answers the question or completes the statement. *PRINT THE LETTER OF THE CORRECT ANSWER IN THE SPACE AT THE RIGHT.*

1. An investigator uses Forms A, B, and C in filling out his investigation reports. He uses Form B five times as often as Form A, and he uses Form C three times as often as Form B.
   If the total number of all forms used by the investigator in a month equal 735, how many times was Form B used? 1.____
   A. 150 B. 175 C. 205 D. 235

2. Of all the investigators in one agency, 25% work in a particular building. Of these, 12% have desks on the 14th floor.
   What percentage of the investigators work in this building but do NOT have desks on the 14th floor? 2.____
   A. 12% B. 13% C. 22% D. 23%

3. An investigator is given two reports to read. Report P is 160 pages long and takes the investigator 3 hours and 20 minutes to read.
   If Report S is 254 pages long and the investigator reads it at the same rate as he reads Report P, how long will it take him to read Report S? _____ hours _____ minutes. 3.____
   A. 4; 15 B. 4; 50 C. 5; 10 D. 5; 30

4. A team of 6 investigators was assigned to interview 234 people.
   If half the investigators conduct twice as many interviews as the other half, and the slow group interviews 12 persons a day, how many days would it take to complete this assignment? _____ days. 4.____
   A. 4½ B. 5 C. 6 D. 6½

5. The investigators in one agency conduct an average of 12 interviews an hour from 10 A.M. to 12 noon and from 1 P.M. to 5 P.M. daily. The director of his agency knows from past experience that 20% of those called in to be interviewed are unable to keep the appointments that were scheduled.
   If the director wants his staff to be kept occupied with interviews for the entire time period that has been set aside for this function, how many appointments should be scheduled for each day? 5.____
   A. 86 B. 90 C. 96 D. 101

6. An investigator has a 430-page report to read. The first day, he is able to read 20 pages. The second day, he reads 10 pages more than the first day, and the third day, he reads 15 pages more than the second day. 6.____

If, on the following days, he continues to read at the same rate as he was reading on the third day, he will complete the report on the _____ day.
A. 7th B. 8th C. 10th D. 11th

7. The 36 investigators in an agency are each required to submit 25 investigation reports a week. These reports are filled out on a certain form, and only one copy of the form is needed per report. 7.____
Allowing 20% for waste, how many packages of 45 forms a piece should be ordered for each weekly period?
A. 15 B. 20 C. 25 D. 30

8. During the fiscal year, an investigative unit received $260 for stationery and telephone expenditures. It spent 43% for stationery and 1/3 of the balance for telephone service. 8.____
The amount of money that was left at the end of the fiscal year was MOST NEARLY
A. $49 B. $50 C. $99 D. $109

Questions 9-10.

DIRECTIONS: Questions 9 and 10 are to be answered SOLELY on the data given below.

Number of days absent per worker (sickness)	1	2	3	4	5	6	7	8 or Over
Number of Workers	96	45	16	3	1	0	1	0
Total Number of Workers:	500							

9. The TOTAL number of man days lost due to illness in 2020 was 9.____
A. 137 B. 154 C. 162 D. 258

10. Of the 500 workers studied, the number who lost NO days due to sickness in 2020 was 10.____
A. 230 B. 298 C. 338 D. 372

Questions 11-13.

DIRECTIONS: Questions 11 through 13 are to be answered SOLELY on the basis of the following passage.

The rise of urban-industrial society has complicated the social arrangements needed to regulate contacts between people. As a consequence, there has been an unprecedented increase in the volume of laws and regulations designed to control individual conduct and to govern the relationship of the individual to others. In a century, there has been an eight-fold increase in the crimes for which one may be prosecuted.

For these offenses, the courts have the ultimate responsibility for redressing wrongs and convicting the guilty. The body of legal precepts gives the impression of an abstract and evenhanded dispensation of justice. Actually, the personnel of the agencies applying these precepts are faced with the difficulties of fitting abstract principles to highly variable situations emerging from the dynamics of everyday life. It is inevitable that discrepancies should exist between precept and practice.

The legal institutions serve as a framework for the social order by their slowness to respond to the caprices of transitory fad. This valuable contribution exacts a price in terms of the inflexibility of legal institutions in responding to new circumstances. This possibility is promoted by the changes in values and norms of the dynamic larger culture of which the legal precepts are a part.

11. According to the above passage, the increase in the number of laws and regulations during the twentieth century can be attributed to the 11.____
    - A. complexity of modern industrial society
    - B. increased seriousness of offenses committed
    - C. growth of individualism
    - D. anonymity of urban living

12. According to the above passage, which of the following presents a problem to the staff of legal agencies? The 12.____
    - A. need to eliminate the discrepancy between precept and practice
    - B. necessity to apply abstract legal precepts to rapidly changing conditions
    - C. responsibility for reducing the number of abstract legal principles
    - D. responsibility for understanding offenses in terms of the real-life situations from which they emerge

13. According to the above passage, it can be concluded that legal institutions affect social institutions by 13.____
    - A. preventing change
    - B. keeping pace with its norms and values
    - C. changing its norms and values
    - D. providing stability

Questions 14-16.

DIRECTIONS: Questions 14 through 16 are to be answered SOLELY on the basis of information given in the following passage.

A personnel interviewer, selecting job applicants, may find that he reacts badly to some people even on first contact. This reaction cannot usually be explained by things that the interviewee has done or said. Most of us have had the experience of liking or disliking, of feeling comfortable and uncomfortable with people on first acquaintance, long before we have had a chance to make a conscious, rational decision about them. Often, too, our liking or disliking is transmitted to the other person by subtle processes such as gestures, posture, voice intonations, or choice of words. The point to be kept in mind is this: the relations between people are complex and occur at several levels, from the conscious to the unconscious. This is true whether the relationship is brief or long, formal or informal.

Some of the major dynamics of personality which operate on the unconscious level are projection, sublimation, rationalization, and repression. Encountering these for the first time, one is apt to think of them as representing pathological states. In the extreme, they undoubtedly are, but they exist so universally that we must consider them also to be parts of normal personality.

Without necessarily subscribing to any of the numerous theories of personality, it is possible to describe personality in terms of certain important aspects or elements. We are all aware of ourselves as thinking organisms.

This aspect of personality, the conscious part, is important for understanding human behavior, but it is not enough. Many find it hard to accept the notion that each person also has an unconscious. The existence of the unconscious is no longer a matter of debate. It is not possible to estimate at all precisely what proportion of our total psychological life is conscious, what proportion unconscious. Everyone who has studied the problem, however, agrees that consciousness is the smaller part of personality. Most of what we are and do is a result of unconscious processes. To ignore this is to risk mistakes.

14. The above passage suggests that an interviewer can be MOST effective if he 14.____
    A. learns how to determine other peoples' unconscious motivations
    B. learns how to repress his own unconsciously motivated mannerisms and behavior
    C. can keep others from feeling that he either likes or dislikes them
    D. gains an understanding of how the unconscious operates in himself and in others

15. It may be inferred from the above passage that the *subtle processes*, such as gestures, posture, voice intonation, or choice of words referred to in the first paragraph are USUALLY 15.____
    A. in the complete control of an expert investigator
    B. the determining factors in the friendships a person establishes
    C. controlled by a person's unconscious
    D. not capable of being consciously controlled

16. The above passage implies that various different personality theories are USUALLY 16.____
    A. so numerous and different as to be valueless to an investigator
    B. in basic agreement about the importance of the unconscious
    C. understood by the investigator who strives to be effective
    D. in agreement that personality factors such as projection and repression are pathological

Questions 17-19.

DIRECTIONS: Questions 17 through 19 are to be answered SOLELY on the basis of information contained in the following passage.

No matter how well the interrogator adjusts himself to the witness and how precisely he induces the witness to describe his observations, mistakes still can be made. The mistakes made by an experienced interrogator may be comparatively few, but as far as the witness is concerned, his path is full of pitfalls. Modern "witness psychology" has shown that even the most honest and trustworthy witnesses are apt to make grave mistakes in good faith. It is, therefore, necessary that the interrogator get an idea of the weak links in the testimony in order to check up on them in the event that something appears to be strange or not quite satisfactory.

Unfortunately, modern witness psychology does not yet offer any means of directly testing the credibility of testimony. It lacks precision and method, in spite of worthwhile attempts on the part of learned men. At the same time, witness psychology, through the gathering of many experience concerning the weaknesses of human testimony, has been of invaluable service. It shows clearly that only evidence of a technical nature has absolute value as proof.

Testimony may be separated into the following stages: (1) perception; (2) observation; (3) mind fixation of the observed occurrences, in which fantasy, association of ideas, and personal judgment participate; (4) expression in oral or written form, where the testimony is transferred from one witness to another or to the interrogator. Each of these stages offers innumerable possibilities for the distortion of testimony.

17. The above passage indicates that having witnesses talk to each other before testifying is a practice which is GENERALLY 17.____
    A. *desirable*, since the witnesses will be able to correct each other's errors in observation before testimony
    B. *undesirable*, since the witnesses will collaborate on one story to tell the investigator
    C. *undesirable*, since one witness may distort his testimony because of what another witness may erroneously say
    D. *desirable*, since witnesses will become aware of discrepancies in their own testimony and can point out the discrepancies to the investigator

18. According to the above passage, the one of the following which would be the MOST reliable for use as evidence would be the testimony of a 18.____
    A. handwriting expert about a signature on a forged check
    B. trained police officer about the identity of a criminal
    C. laboratory technician about an accident he has observed
    D. psychologist who has interviewed any witness who relate conflicting stories

19. Concerning the validity of evidence, it is clear from the above passage that 19.____
    A. only evidence of a technical nature is at all valuable
    B. the testimony of witnesses is so flawed that it is usually valueless
    C. an investigator, by knowing modern witness psychology, will usually be able to perceive mistaken testimony
    D. an investigator ought to expect mistakes in even the most reliable witness testimony

Questions 20-21.

DIRECTIONS: Questions 20 and 21 are to be answered SOLELY on the basis of information given in the following passage.

Since we generally assure informants that what they say is confidential, we are not free to tell one informant what the other has told us. Even if the informant says, "*I don't care who knows it; tell anybody you want to*," we find it wise to treat the interview as confidential. An interviewer who relates to some informants what other informants have told him is likely to stir up anxiety and suspicion. Of course, the interviewer may be able to tell an informant what he has heard without revealing the source of his information. This may be perfectly appropriate where a story has wide currency so that an informant cannot infer the source of the information. But if an event is not widely known, the mere mention of it may reveal to one informant what another informant has said about the situation. How can the data be cross-checked in these circumstances.

20. The above passage IMPLIES that the anxiety and suspicion an interviewer may arouse by telling what has been learned in other interviews is due to the 20.____
    A. lack of trust the person interviewed may have in the interviewer's honesty
    B. troublesome nature of the material which the interviewer has learned in other interviews
    C. fact that the person interviewed may not believe that permission was given to repeat the information
    D. fear of the person interviewed that what he is telling the interviewer will be repeated

21. The above passage is MOST likely part of a longer passage dealing with 21.____
    A. ways to verify data gathered in interviews
    B. the various anxieties a person being interviewed may feel
    C. the notion that people sometimes say things they do not mean
    D. ways an interview can avoid seeming suspicious

Questions 22-23.

DIRECTIONS: Questions 22 and 23 are to be answered SOLELY on the basis of information given below.

The ability to interview rests not on any single trait, but on a vast complex of them. Habits, skills, techniques, and attitudes are all involved. Competence in interviewing is acquired only after careful and diligent study, prolonged practice (preferably under supervision), and a good bit of trial and error; for interviewing is not an exact science; it is an art. Like many other arts, however, it can and must draw on science in several of its aspects.

There is always a place for individual initiative, for imaginative innovations, and for new combinations of old approaches. The skilled interviewer cannot be bound by a set of rules. Likewise, there is not a set of rules which can guarantee to the novice that his interviewing will be successful. There are, however, some accepted, general guideposts which may help the beginner to avoid mistakes, learn how to conserve this efforts, and establish effective working relationships with interviewees; to accomplish, in short, what he sets out to do.

22. According to the above passage, rules and standard techniques for interviewing are 22.____
    A. helpful for the beginner, but useless for the experienced, innovative interviewer
    B. destructive of the innovation and initiative needed for a good interviewer
    C. useful for even the experienced interviewer who may, however, sometimes go beyond them
    D. the means by which nearly anybody can become an effective interviewer

23. According to the above passage, the one of the following which is a prerequisite to competent interviewing is 23.____
    A. avoid mistakes
    B. study and practice
    C. imaginative innovation
    D. natural aptitude

Questions 24-27.

DIRECTIONS: Questions 24 through 27 are to be answered SOLELY on the basis of information given in the following passage.

The question of what material is relevant is not as simple as it might seem. Frequently, material which seems irrelevant to the inexperienced has, because of the common tendency to disguise and distort and misplace one's feelings, considerable significance. It may be necessary to let the client "ramble on" for a while in order to clear the decks, as it were, so that he may get down to things that really are on his mind. On the other hand, with an already disturbed person, it may be important for the interviewer to know when to discourage further elaboration of upsetting material. This is especially the case where the worker would be unable to do anything about it. An inexperienced interviewer might, for instance, be intrigued with the bizarre elaboration of material that the psychotic produces, but further elaboration of this might encourage the client in his instability. A too random discussion may indicate that the interviewee is not certain in what areas the interviewer is prepared to help him, and he may be seeking some direction. Or again, satisfying though it may be for the interviewer to have the interviewee tell him intimate details, such revelations sometimes need to be checked or encouraged only in small doses. An interviewee who has "talked too much" often reveals subsequent anxiety. This is illustrated by the fact that frequently after a "confessional" interview, the interviewee surprises the interviewer by being withdrawn, inarticulate, or hostile, or by breaking the next appointment.

24. Sometimes a client may reveal certain personal information to an interviewer and subsequently may feel anxious about this revelation. 24.____
    If, during an interview, a client begins to discuss very personal matters, it would be BEST to
    A. tell the client, in no uncertain terms, that you're not interested in personal details
    B. ignore the client at this point
    C. encourage the client to elaborate further on the details
    D. inform the client that the information seems to be very personal

25. The author indicates that clients with severe psychological disturbances pose an especially difficult problem for the inexperienced interviewer. 25.____
The difficulty lies in the possibility of the client
    A. becoming physically violent and harming the interviewer
    B. rambling on for a while
    C. revealing irrelevant details which may be followed by cancelled appointments
    D. reverting to an unstable state as a result of interview material

26. An interviewer should be constantly alert to the possibility of obtaining clues from the client as to the problem areas. 26.____
According to the above passage, a client who discusses topics at random may be
    A. unsure of what problems the interviewer can provide help with
    B. reluctant to discuss intimate details
    C. trying to impress the interviewer with his knowledge
    D. deciding what relevant material to elaborate on

27. The evaluation of a client's responses may reveal substantial information that may aid the interviewer in assessing the problem areas that are of concern to the client. Responses that seemed irrelevant at the time of the interview may be of significance because 27.____
    A. considerable significance is attached to all relevant material
    B. emotional feelings are frequently masked
    C. an initial *rambling on* is often a prelude to what is actually bothering the client
    D. disturbed clients often reveal subsequent anxiety

Questions 28-30.

DIRECTIONS: Questions 28 through 30 are to be answered SOLELY on the basis of the following passage.

The physical setting of the interview may determine its entire potentiality. Some degree of privacy and a comfortable relaxed atmosphere are important. The interviewee is not encouraged to give much more than his name and address if the interviewer seems busy with other things, if people are rushing about, if there are distracting noises. He has a right to feel that, whether the interview lasts five minutes or an hour, he has, for that time, the undivided attention of the interviewer. Interruptions, telephone calls, and so on, should be reduced to a minimum. If the interviewee has waited in a crowded room for what seems to him an interminably long period, he is naturally in mood to sit down and discuss what is on his mind. Indeed, by that time, the primary thing on his mind may be his irritation at being kept waiting, and he frequently feels it would be impolite to express this. If a wait or interruptions have been unavoidable, it is always helpful to give the client some recognition that these are disturbing and that we can naturally understand that they make it more difficult for him to proceed. At the same time, if he protests that they have not troubled him, the interviewer can best accept his statements at their face value, as further insistence that they must have been disturbing may be interpreted by him as accusing, and he may conclude that the interviewer has been personally hurt by his irritation.

28. Distraction during an interview may tend to limit the client's responses. In a case where an interruption has occurred, it would be BEST for the investigator to 28.____
    A. terminate this interview and have it rescheduled for another time period
    B. ignore the interruption since it is not continuous
    C. express his understanding that the distraction can cause the client to feel disturbed
    D. accept the client's protests that he has been troubled by the interruption

29. To maximize the rapport that can be established with the client, an appropriate physical setting is necessary. At the very least, some privacy would be necessary. In addition, the interviewer should 29.____
    A. always appear to be busy in order to impress the client
    B. focus his attention only on the client
    C. accept all the client's statements as being valid
    D. stress the importance of the interview to the client

30. Clients who have been waiting quite some time for their interview may, justifiably, become upset. However, a client may initially attempt to mask these feelings because he may 30.____
    A. personally hurt the interviewer
    B. want to be civil
    C. feel that the wait was unavoidable
    D. fear the consequences of his statement

KEY (CORRECT ANSWERS)

1.	B	11.	A	21.	A
2.	C	12.	B	22.	C
3.	D	13.	D	23.	B
4.	D	14.	D	24.	D
5.	B	15.	C	25.	D
6.	D	16.	B	26.	A
7.	C	17.	C	27.	B
8.	C	18.	A	28.	C
9.	D	19.	D	29.	B
10.	C	20.	D	30.	B

TEST 2

DIRECTIONS: Each question or incomplete statement is followed by several suggested answers or completions. Select the one that BEST answers the question or completes the statement. *PRINT THE LETTER OF THE CORRECT ANSWER IN THE SPACE AT THE RIGHT.*

Questions 1-5.

DIRECTIONS: In Questions 1 through 5, choose the statement which is BEST from the point of view of English usage suitable for a business report.

1. A. The client's receiving of public assistance checks at two different addresses were disclosed by the investigation. 1.____
   B. The investigation disclosed that the client was receiving public assistance checks at two different addresses.
   C. The client was found out by the investigator to be receiving public assistance checks at two different addresses.
   D. The client has been receiving public assistance checks at two different addresses, disclosed the investigation

2. A. The investigation of complaints are usually handled by this unit, which deals with internal security problems in the department. 2.____
   B. This unit deals with internal security problems in the department; usually investigating complaints.
   C. Investigating complaints is this unit's job, being that it handles internal security problems in the department
   D. This unit deals with internal security problems in the department and usually investigates complaints.

3. A. The delay in completing this investigation was caused by difficulty in obtaining the required documents from the candidate. 3.____
   B. Because of difficulty in obtaining the required documents from the candidate is the reason that there was a delay in completing this investigation.
   C. Having had difficulty in obtaining the required documents from the candidate, there was a delay in completing this investigation.
   D. Difficulty in obtaining the required documents from the candidate had the affect of delaying the completion of this investigation.

4. A. This report, together with documents supporting our recommendation, are being submitted for your approval. 4.____
   B. Documents supporting our recommendation is being submitted with the report for your approval.
   C. This report, together with documents supporting our documentation, is being submitted for your approval.
   D. The report and documents supporting our recommendation is being submitted for your approval.

5. A. Several people were interviewed and numerous letters were sent before this case was completed. 5.____
   B. Completing this case, interviewing several people and sending numerous letters were necessary.
   C. To complete this case needed interviewing several people and sending numerous letters.
   D. Interviewing several people and sending numerous letters was necessary to complete the case.

Questions 6-20.

DIRECTIONS: For each of the sentences numbered 6 to 20, select from the options given below the MOST applicable choice, and mark your answer accordingly.
A. The sentence is correct.
B. The sentence contains a spelling error only.
C. The sentence contains an English grammar error only.
D. The sentence contains both a spelling error and an English grammar error.

6. He is a very dependible person whom we expect will be an asset to this division. 6.____

7. An investigator often finds it necessary to be very diplomatic when conducting an interview. 7.____

8. Accurate detail is especially important if court action results from an investigation. 8.____

9. The report was signed by him and I since we conducted the investigation jointly. 9.____

10. Upon receipt of the complaint, an inquiry was begun. 10.____

11. An employee has to organize his time so that he can handle his workload efficiantly. 11.____

12. It was not apparent that anyone was living at the address given by the client. 12.____

13. According to regulations, there is to be at least three attempts made to locate the client. 13.____

14. Neither the inmate nor the correction officer was willing to sign a formal statement. 14.____

15. It is our opinion that one of the persons interviewed were lying. 15.____

16. We interviewed both clients and departmental personel in the course of this investigation. 16.____

17. It is concievable that further research might produce additional evidence. 17.____

18. There are too many occurences of this nature to ignore. 18.____

19. We cannot accede to the candidate's request. 19.____

20. The submission of overdue reports is the reason that there was a delay in completion of this investigation. 20.____

Questions 21-2.

DIRECTIONS: Each of Questions 21 through 25 consists of three sentences lettered A, B, and C. In each of these questions, one of the sentences may contain an error in grammar, sentence structure, or punctuation, or all three sentences may be correct. If one of the sentences in a question contains an error in grammar, sentence structure, or punctuation, print in the space at the right the capital letter preceding the sentence which contains the error. If all three sentences are correct, print the letter D.

21. A. Mr. Smith appears to be less competent than I in performing these duties. 21.____
    B. The supervisor spoke to the employee, who had made the error, but did not reprimand him.
    C. When he found the book lying on the table, he immediately notified the owner.

22. A. Being locked in the desk, we were certain that the papers would not be taken. 22.____
    B. It wasn't I who dictated the telegram; I believe it was Eleanor.
    C. You should interview whoever comes to the office today.

23. A. The clerk was instructed to set the machine on the table before summoning the manager. 23.____
    B. He said that he was not familiar with those kind of activities.
    C. A box of pencils, in addition to erasers and blotters, was included in the shipment.

24. A. The supervisor remarked, "Assigning an employee to the proper type of work is not always easy." 24.____
    B. The employer found that each of the applicants were qualified to perform the duties of the position.
    C. Any competent student is permitted to take this course if he obtains the consent of the instructor.

25. A. The prize was awarded to the employee whom the judges believed to be most deserving. 25.____
    B. Since the instructor believes this book is the better of the two, he is recommending it for use in the school.
    C. It was obvious to the employees that the completion of the task by the scheduled date would require their working overtime.

KEY (CORRECT ANSWERS)

1.	B	11.	B
2.	D	12.	B
3.	A	13.	C
4.	C	14.	A
5.	A	15.	C
6.	D	16.	B
7.	A	17.	B
8.	A	18.	B
9.	C	19.	A
10.	A	20.	C

21.	B
22.	A
23.	B
24.	B
25.	D

READING COMPREHENSION
UNDERSTANDING AND INTERPRETING WRITTEN MATERIAL
EXAMINATION SECTION
TEST 1

DIRECTIONS: Each question or incomplete statement is followed by several suggested answers or completions. Select the one that BEST answers the question or completes the statement. *PRINT THE LETTER OF THE CORRECT ANSWER IN THE SPACE AT THE RIGHT.*

Questions 1-3.

DIRECTIONS: Questions 1 through 3 are to be answered SOLELY on the basis of the following paragraph.

The aging housing inventory presents a broad spectrum of conditions, from good upkeep to unbelievable deterioration. Buildings, even relatively good buildings, are likely to have numerous minor violations rather than the gross and evident sanitary violations of an earlier age. Except for the serious violations in a relatively small number of slum buildings, the task is to deal with masses of minor violations that, though insignificant in themselves, amount in the aggregate to major deprivations of health and comfort to tenants. Caused by wear and tear, by the abrasions of time, and aggravated by neglect, these conditions do not readily yield to the dramatic *vacate and restore* measures of earlier times. Moreover, the lines between *good* and *bad* housing have become blurred in many parts of our cities; we find a range of *shades of gray* blending into each other. Different kinds of code enforcement efforts may be required to deal with different degrees of deterioration.

1. The above passage suggests that code enforcement efforts may have to be 1.____

   A. developed to cope with varying levels of housing dilapidation
   B. aimed primarily at the serious violations in slum buildings
   C. modeled on the *vacate and restore* measures of earlier times
   D. modified to reduce unrealistic penalties for petty violations

2. According to the above passage, during former times some buildings had sanitary violations which were 2.____

   A. irreparable and minor
   B. blurred and gray
   C. flagrant and obvious
   D. insignificant and numerous

3. According to the above passage, the aging housing stock presents a 3.____

   A. great number of rent-controlled buildings
   B. serious problem of tenant-caused deterioration
   C. significant increase in buildings without intentional violations
   D. wide range of physical conditions

Questions 4-5.

DIRECTIONS: Questions 4 and 5 are to be answered SOLELY on the basis of the following passage.

In general, housing code provisions relating to the safe and sanitary maintenance of dwelling units prescribe the maintenance required for foundations, walls, ceilings, floors, windows, doors, stairways, and also the facilities and equipment required in other sections. The more recent codes have, in addition, extensive provisions designed to ensure that the unit be maintained in a rat-free and rat-proof condition. Also, as an example of new approaches in code provisions, one proposed Federal model housing code prohibits the landlord from terminating vital services and utilities except during temporary emergencies or when actual repairs or maintenance are in process. This provision may be used to prevent a landlord from turning off utility services as a technique of self-help eviction or as a weapon against rent strikes.

4. According to the above passage, the more recent housing codes have extensive provisions designed to 4.____

   A. maintain a reasonably fire-proof living unit
   B. prohibit tenants from participating in rent strikes
   C. maintain the unit free from rats
   D. prohibit tenants from using lead-based paints

5. According to the above passage, one housing code would permit landlords to terminate vital services during 5.____

   A. a rent strike
   B. an actual eviction
   C. a temporary emergency
   D. the planning of repairs and maintenance

Questions 6-8.

DIRECTIONS: Questions 6 through 8 are to be answered SOLELY on the basis of the following passage.

City governments have long had building codes which set minimum standards for building and for human occupancy. The code (or series of codes) makes provisions for standards of lighting and ventilation, sanitation, fire prevention, and protection. As a result of demands from manufacturers, builders, real estate people, tenement owners, and building-trades unions, these codes often have established minimum standards well below those that the contemporary society would accept as a rock-bottom minimum. Codes often become outdated so that meager standards in one era become seriously inadequate a few decades later as society"s concept of a minimum standard of living changes. Out-of-date codes, when still in use, have sometimes prevented the introduction of new devices and modern building techniques. Thus, it is extremely important that building codes keep pace with changes in the accepted concept of a minimum standard of living.

6. According to the above passage, all of the following considerations in building planning would probably be covered in a building code EXCEPT 6.____

   A. closet space as a percentage of total floor area
   B. size and number of windows required for rooms of differing sizes
   C. placement of fire escapes in each line of apartments
   D. type of garbage disposal units to be installed

7. According to the above passage, if an ideal building code were to be created, how would the established minimum standards in it compare to the ones that are presently set by city governments? 7.____
   They would

   A. be lower than they are at present
   B. be higher than they are at present
   C. be comparable to the present minimum standards
   D. vary according to the economic group that sets them

8. On the basis of the above passage, what is the reason for difficulties in introducing new building techniques? 8.____

   A. Builders prefer techniques which represent the rock-bottom minimum desired by society.
   B. Certain manufacturers have obtained patents on various building methods to the exclusion of new techniques.
   C. The government does not want to invest money in techniques that will soon be outdated.
   D. New techniques are not provided for in building codes which are not up-to-date.

Questions 9-11.

DIRECTIONS: Questions 9 through 11 are to be answered SOLELY on the basis of the following paragraph.

When constructed within a multiple dwelling, such storage space shall be equipped with a sprinkler system and also with a system of mechanical ventilation in no way connected with any other ventilating system. Such storage space shall have no opening into any other part of the dwelling except through a fireproof vestibule. Any such vestibule shall have a minimum superficial floor area of fifty square feet, and its maximum area shall not exceed seventy-five square feet. It shall be enclosed with incombustible partitions having a fire-resistive rating of three hours. The floor and ceiling of such vestibule shall also be of incombustible material having a fire-resistive rating of at least three hours. There shall be two doors to provide access from the dwelling,to the car storage space. Each such door shall have a fire-resistive rating of one and one-half hours and shall be provided with a device to prevent the opening of one door until the other door is entirely closed.

9. According to the above paragraph, the one of the following that is REQUIRED in order for cars to be permitted to be stored in a multiple dwelling is a(n) 9.____

   A. fireproof vestibule
   B. elevator from the garage
   C. approved heating system
   D. sprinkler system

10. According to the above paragraph, the one of the following materials that would NOT be acceptable for the walls of a vestibule connecting a garage to the dwelling portion of a building is 10.____

A. 3" solid gypsum blocks
B. 4" brick
C. 4" hollow gypsum blocks, plastered both sides
D. 6" solid cinder concrete blocks

11. According to the above paragraph, the one of the following that would be ACCEPTABLE for the width and length of a vestibule connecting a garage that is within a multiple dwelling to the dwelling portion of the building is 11.____

A. 3'8" x 13'0"
B. 4'6" x 18'6"
C. 4'9" x 14'6"
D. 4'3" x 19'3"

Questions 12-13.

DIRECTIONS: Questions 12 and 13 are to be answered SOLELY on the basis of the following paragraph.

It shall be unlawful to place, use, or maintain in a condition intended, arranged, or designed for use, any gas-fired cooking appliance, laundry stove, heating stove, range or water heater or combination of such appliances in any room or space used for living or sleeping in any new or existing multiple dwelling unless such room or space has a window opening to the outer air or such gas appliance is vented to the outer air. All automatically operated gas appliances shall be equipped with a device which shall shut off automatically the gas supply to the main burners when the pilot light in such appliance is extinguished. A gas range or the cooking portion of a gas appliance incorporating a room heater shall not be deemed an automatically operated gas appliance. However, burners in gas ovens and broilers which can be turned on and off or ignited by non-manual means shall be equipped with a device which shall shut off automatically the gas supply to those burners when the operation of such non-manual means fails.

12. According to the above paragraph, an automatic shut-off device is NOT required on a gas 12.____

A. hot water heater
B. laundry dryer
C. space heater
D. range

13. According to the above paragraph, a gas-fired water heater is permitted 13.____

A. only in kitchens
B. only in bathrooms
C. only in living rooms
D. in any type of room

Questions 14-18.

DIRECTIONS: Questions 14 through 18 are to be answered SOLELY on the basis of the information contained in the statement below.

No multiple dwelling shall be erected to a height in excess of one and one-half times the width of the widest street on which it faces, except that above the level of such height, for each one foot that the front wall of such dwelling sets back from the street line, three feet shall be added to the height limit of such dwelling, but such dwelling shall not exceed in maximum height three feet plus one and three-quarter times the width of the widest street on which it faces.

Any such dwelling facing a street more than one hundred feet in width shall be subject to the same height limitations as though such dwelling faced a street one hundred feet in width.

14. The MAXIMUM height of a multiple dwelling set back five feet from the street line and facing a 60 foot wide street is feet. 14.____

A. 60 B. 90 C. 105 D. 165

15. The MAXIMUM height of a multiple dwelling set back six feet from the street line and facing a 120 foot wide street is ______ feet. 15.____

A. 198 B. 168 C. 120 D. 105

16. The MAXIMUM height of a multiple dwelling is 16.____

A. 100 ft. B. 150 ft. C. 178 ft. D. unlimited

17. The MAXIMUM height of a multiple dwelling set back 10 feet from the street line and facing a 110 foot wide street is feet. 17.____

A. 178 B. 180 C. 195 D. 205

18. The MAXIMUM height of a multiple dwelling set back eight feet from the street line and facing a 90 foot wide street is feet. 18.____

A. 135 B. 147 C. 178 D. 159

Questions 19-23.

DIRECTIONS: Questions 19 through 23 are to be answered SOLELY on the basis of the following statement.

The number of persons accommodated on any story in a lodging house shall not be greater than the sum of the following components,

a. 22 persons for each full multiple of 22 inches in the smallest clear width for each means of egress approved by the department, other than fire escapes
b. 20 persons for each lawful fire escape accessible from such story.

19. The MAXIMUM number of persons that may be accommodated on a story in a lodging house depends on the 19.____

A. number of lawful fire escapes *only*
B. number of approved means of egress *only*
C. smallest clear width in each approved means of egress *only*
D. number of lawful fire escapes and sum total of smallest clear widths in each approved means of egress

20. The MAXIMUM number of persons that may be accommodated on a story of a lodging house having one lawful fire escape and a sum total of 44 inches in the smallest clear widths of the two approved means of egress is 20.____

A. 20 B. 22 C. 42 D. 64

21. The MAXIMUM number of persons that may be accommodated on a story of a lodging house having two lawful fire escapes and a sum total of 60 inches in the smallest clear width of the approved means of egress is 21.____

A. 64 B. 84 C. 100 D. 106

22. The MAXIMUM number of persons that may be accommodated on a story of a lodging house having one lawful fire escape and a sum total of 33 inches in the smallest clear width of the approved means of egress is 22.____

A. 42 B. 53 C. 64 D. 73

23. The MAXIMUM number of persons that may be accommodated on a story of a lodging house having two lawful fire escapes and two approved means of egress, with 40 inches and 44 inches in the smallest clear widths, respectively, is 23.____

A. 84 B. 104 C. 106 D. 108

Questions 24-25.

DIRECTIONS: Questions 24 and 25 are to be answered SOLELY on the basis of the following paragraph.

Though the recent trend toward apartment construction may appear to be the Region's response to large-lot zoning and centralized industry, it really is not. It is mainly a function of the age of the population. Most of the apartments are occupied by one- and two-person families young people out of school but without a family of their own and older people whose children have grown. Both groups have been increasing in number; and, in this Region, they characteristically live in apartments. It is this increased demand for apartments and the simultaneous decrease in demand for one-family houses that dramatically raised the percentage of building permits issued for multi-family housing units from 36 percent in 1977 to 67 percent in 1981. The fact that three-fourths of the apartments were built in the Core between 1977 and 1981 at the same time as the Core was losing population underscores the failure of the apartment boom to slow the outward spread of the population.

24. According to the above paragraph, one of the reasons for the increase in the number of building permits issued for multi-family construction in the City Metropolitan Region is 24.____

A. that workers in industry want to live close to their jobs
B. an increase in the number of elderly people living in the Region
C. the inability of many families to afford the large lots necessary to build private homes
D. the new zoning ordinance made it easier to build apartments

25. According to the above paragraph, the apartment construction boom 25.____

A. increased the population density in the Core
B. spurred a population shift to the suburbs
C. did not halt the outward flow of the population from the Core
D. was most significant in the outer areas of the Region

KEY (CORRECT ANSWERS)

1. A
2. C
3. D
4. C
5. C
6. A
7. B
8. D
9. D
10. B
11. C
12. D
13. D
14. C
15. B
16. C
17. A
18. D
19. D
20. D
21. B
22. A
23. C
24. B
25. C

TEST 2

DIRECTIONS: Each question or incomplete statement is followed by several suggested answers or completions. Select the one that BEST answers the question or completes the statement. *PRINT THE LETTER OF THE CORRECT ANSWER IN THE SPACE AT THE RIGHT.*

Questions 1-4.

DIRECTIONS: Questions 1 through 4 are to be answered SOLELY on the basis of the following paragraph.

Although the suburbs have provided housing and employment for millions of additional families since 1950, many suburban communities have maintained controls over the kinds of families who can live in them. Suburban attitudes have been formed by reaction against a perception of crowded, harassed city life and threatening alien city people. As population, taxable income, and jobs have left the cities for the suburbs, the *urban crisis* of substandard housing, declining levels of education and public services, and decreasing employment opportunities has been created. The crisis, however, is not urban at all, but national, and in part a result of the suburban policy that discourages outward movement by the urban poor.

1. According to the above paragraph, the quality of urban life 1.____

   A. is determined by public opinion in the cities
   B. has worsened in recent years
   C. is similar to rural life
   D. can be changed by political means

2. According to the above paragraph, suburban communities have 2.____

   A. tried to show that the urban crisis is really a national crisis
   B. avoided taking a position on the urban crisis
   C. been involved in causing the urban crisis
   D. been the innocent victims of the urban crisis

3. According to the above paragraph, the poor have 3.____

   A. become increasingly sophisticated in their attempts to move to the suburbs
   B. generally been excluded from the suburbs
   C. lost incentive for betterment of their living conditions
   D. sought improvement of the central cities

4. As used in the above paragraph, the word perception means MOST NEARLY 4.____

   A. development
   B. impression
   C. opposition
   D. uncertainty

Questions 5-8.

DIRECTIONS: Questions 5 through 8 are to be answered SOLELY on the basis of the following paragraph.

The concentration of publicly assisted housing in central cities -- because the suburbs do not want them and effectively bar them -- is usually rationalized by a solicitous regard for keeping intact the city neighborhoods cherished by low-income groups. If one accepted this as valid, the devotion of minorities to blighted city neighborhoods in preference to suburban employment and housing would be an historic first. Certainly no such devotion was visible among the millions who have deserted their city neighborhoods in the last 25 years even if it meant an arduous daily trip from the suburbs to their jobs in the cities.

5. The writer implies that MOST poor people 5.____

A. prefer isolation
B. fear change
C. are angry
D. seek betterment

6. The general tone of the paragraph is BEST characterized as 6.____

A. uncertain
B. skeptical
C. evasive
D. indifferent

7. As used in the above paragraph, the word <u>rationalize</u> means MOST NEARLY 7.____

A. dispute
B. justify
C. deny
D. locate

8. According to the above paragraph, publicly assisted housing is concentrated in the central cities PRIMARILY because 8.____

A. city dwellers are unable to find satisfactory housing
B. deterioration of older housing has increased in recent years
C. suburbanites have opposed the movement of the poor to the suburbs
D. employment opportunities have decreased in the suburbs

Questions 9-11.

DIRECTIONS: Questions 9 through 11 are to be answered SOLELY on the basis of the following paragraph.

In recent years, new and important emphasis has been placed upon the maximum use of conservation and rehabilitation techniques in carrying out programs of urban renewal and revitalization. In urban renewal projects where existing structures are hopelessly deteriorated or land uses are incompatible with the community's overall plans, the entire area may be acquired, cleared, and sold for redevelopment. However, where existing structures are basically sound but have deteriorated to the point where they are a <u>blighting</u> influence on the neighborhood, they may be salvaged through a program of rehabilitation and reconditioning.

9. According to the above paragraph, the one of the following which is MOST likely to cause area-wide razing of the buildings in urban renewal programs is 9.____

A. a program of rehabilitation and reconditioning
B. concerted insistence by landlords and tenants that certain buildings be bulldozed
C. an inability of community groups to agree on priorities for staged clearance
D. land use contrary to the community's general plan

10. According to the above paragraph, rehabilitation of structures may take place if 10.____

A. new conservation and rehabilitation techniques are used
B. salvaging all the buildings in the entire area is hopeless
C. the community wishes to preserve historic structures
D. the existing buildings are structurally sound

11. As used in the above paragraph, the word <u>blighting</u> means MOST NEARLY 11.____

A. ruining B. infrequent C. recurrent D. traditional

Questions 12-13.

DIRECTIONS: Questions 12 and 13 are to be answered SOLELY on the basis of the following paragraphs.

We must also find better ways to handle the relocation of people uprooted by projects. In the past, many renewal plans have foundered on this problem, and it is still the most difficult part of the community development. Large-scale replacement of low-income residents -- many ineligible for public housing -- has contributed to deterioration of surrounding communities. However, thanks to changes in housing authority procedures, relocation has been accomplished in a far more satisfactory fashion. The step-by-step community development projects we advocate in this plan should bring further improvement.

But additional measures will be necessary. There are going to be more people to be moved; and, with the current shortage of apartments, large ones especially, it is going to be tougher to find places to move them to. The city should have more freedom to buy or lease housing that comes on the market because of normal turnover and make it available to relocatees.

12. According to the above paragraphs, one of the reasons a neighborhood may deteriorate is that 12.____

A. there is a scarcity of large apartments
B. step-by-step community development projects have failed
C. people in the given neighborhood are uprooted from their homes
D. a nearby renewal project has an inadequate relocation plan

13. From the above paragraphs, one might conclude that the relocation phase of community renewal has been improved. 13.____

A. by changes in housing authority procedures
B. by development of step-by-step community development projects
C. through expanded city powers to buy housing for relocation
D. by the addition of huge sums of money

Questions 14-15.

DIRECTIONS: Questions 14 and 15 are to be answered SOLELY on the basis of the following paragraphs.

Provision of decent housing for the lower half of the population (by income) was thus taken on as a public responsibility. Public housing was to assist the poorest quarter of urban families while the 221(d)(3) Housing Program would assist the next quarter. But limited funds meant that the supply of subsidized housing could not stretch nearly far enough to help this half of the population. Who were to be left out in the rationing process which was accomplished by the sifting of applicants for housing on the part of public and private authorities?

Discrimination on the grounds of race or color is not allowed under Federal law. In all sections of the country, encouragingly, housing programs are found which follow this law to the letter. Yet, housing programs in some cities still suffer from the residue of racial segregation policies and attitudes that for years were condoned or even encouraged.

Some sifting in the 221(d)(3) Housing Program follows the practice of many public housing authorities, the imposition of requirements with respect to character. This is a delicate matter. To fill a project overwhelmingly with broken families, alcoholics, criminals, delinquents, and other problem tenants would hardly make it a wholesome environment. Yet the total exclusion of such families is hardly an acceptable alternative. To the extent this exclusion is practiced, the very people whose lives are described in order to persuade lawmakers and the public to instigate new programs find the door shut in their faces when such programs come into being. The proper balance is difficult to achieve, but society's neediest families surely should not be totally denied the opportunities for rejuvenation in subsidized housing.

14. From the above paragraphs, it can be assumed that the 221(d)(3) Housing Program 14.____

A. served a population earning more than the median income
B. served a less affluent population than is served by public housing
C. excludes all problem families from its projects
D. is a subsidized housing program

15. According to this text, the provision of housing for the poor 15.____

A. has not been completely accomplished with public monies
B. is never influenced by segregationist policies
C. is limited to providing housing for only the neediest families
D. is primarily the responsibility of the Federal government

16. Five hundred persons attended a public hearing at which a proposed public housing project was being considered. Less than half favored the project while the majority opposed the project. 16.____
According to the above statement, it is REASONABLE to conclude that

A. the proposal stimulated considerable community interest
B. the public housing project was disapproved by the city because a majority opposed it
C. those who opposed the project lacked sympathy for needy persons
D. the supporters of the project were led by militants

17. A vacant lot close to a polluted creek is for sale. Two buyers compete. One owns an adjacent factory which provides 300 high paying unskilled jobs. He needs to expand or move from the city. If he expands, he will provide 300 additional jobs. The other is a community group in a changing residential area close by. They hope to stabilize the neighborhood by bringing in new housing. They would build an apartment building with 100 dwelling units on the lot. 17.____
According to the above paragraph, it is REASONABLE to conclude that

A. jobs are more important than housing
B. there is conflict between the factory owners and the neighborhood group
C. the neighborhood group will not succeed in stabilizing the area by constructing new housing
D. the polluted creek should be cleaned up

18. The housing authority faces every problem of the private developer, and it must also assume responsibilities of which private building is free. The authority must account to the community; it must conform to federal regulations; it must provide durable buildings of good standard at low cost; it must overcome the prejudices against public operations, of contractors, bankers, and prospective tenants. These authorities are being watched by anti-housing enthusiasts for the first error of judgment or the first evidence of high costs, to be torn to bits before a Congressional committee. 18.____
On the basis of this statement, it would be MOST correct to state that

A. private builders do not have the opposition of contractors, bankers, and prospective tenants
B. Congressional committees impede the progress of public housing by petty investigations
C. a housing authority must deal with all the difficulties encountered by the private builder
D. housing authorities are no more immune from errors in judgment than private developers

19. Another factor that has considerably added to the city's housing crisis has been the great influx of low-income workers and their families seeking better employment opportunities during wartime and defense boom periods. The circumstances of these families have forced them to crowd into the worst kind of housing and have produced on a renewed scale the conditions from which slums flourish and grow. 19.____
On the basis of this statement, one would be justified in stating that

A. the influx of low-income workers has aggravated the slum problem
B. the city has better employment opportunities than other sections of the country
C. the high wages paid by our defense industries have made many families ineligible for tenancy in public housing projects
D. the families who settled in the city during wartime and the defense build-up brought with them language and social customs conducive to the growth of slums

20. Much of the city felt the effects of the general postwar increase of vandalism and street crime, and the greatly expanded public housing program was no exception. Projects built in congested slum areas with a high incidence of delinquency and crime were particularly subjected to the depredations of neighborhood gangs. The civil service watchmen who patrolled the projects, unarmed and neither trained nor expected to perform police duties, were unable to cope with the situation. 20.____
On the basis of this statement, the MOST accurate of the following statements is:

A. Neighborhood gangs were particularly responsible for the high incidence of delinquency and crime in congested slum areas having public housing programs
B. Civil service watchmen who patrolled housing projects failed to carry out their assigned police duties
C. Housing projects were not spared the effects of the general postwar increase of vandalism and street crime
D. Delinquency and crime affected housing projects in slum areas to a greater extent than other dwellings in the same area

21. Another peculiar characteristic of real estate is the absence of liquidity. Each parcel is a discrete unit as to size, location, rental, physical condition, and financing arrangements. Each property requires investigation, comparison of rents with other properties, and individualized haggling on price and terms. 21.____
On the basis of this statement, the LEAST accurate of the following statements is:

A. Although the size, location, and rent of parcels vary, comparison with rents of other properties affords an indication of the value of a particular parcel
B. Bargaining skill is the essential factor in determining the value of a parcel of real estate
C. Each parcel of real estate has individual peculiarities distinguishing it from any other parcel
D. Real estate is not easily converted to other types of assets

22. In part, at least, the charges of sameness, monotony, and institutionalism directed at public housing projects result from the degree in which they differ from the city's normal housing pattern. They seem alike because their very difference from the usual makes them stand apart. 22.____
In many respects, there is considerably more variety between public housing projects than there is between different streets of apartment houses or tenements throughout the city.
On the basis of this statement, it would be LEAST accurate to state that:

A. There is considerably more variety between public housing projects than there is between different streets of tenements throughout the city
B. Public housing projects differ from the city's normal housing pattern to the degree that sameness, monotony, and institutionalism are characteristic of public buildings
C. Public housing projects seem alike because their deviation from the usual dwellings draws attention to them
D. The variety in structure between public housing projects and other public buildings is related to the period in which they were built

23. The amount of debt that can be charged against the city for public housing is limited by law. Part of the city's restricted housing means goes for cash subsidies it may be required to contribute to state-aided projects. Under the provisions of the state law, the city must match the state's contributions in subsidies; and while the value of the partial tax exemption granted by the city is counted for this purpose, it is not always sufficient. 23.____
On the basis of this statement, it would be MOST accurate to state that:

A. The amount of money the city may spend for public housing is limited by annual tax revenues
B. The value of tax exemptions granted by the city to educational, religious, and charitable institutions may be added to its subsidy contributions to public housing projects
C. The subsidy contributions for state-aided public housing projects are shared equally by the state and the city under the provisions of the state law
D. The tax revenues of the city, unless supplemented by state aid, are insufficient to finance public housing projects

24. Maintenance costs can be minimized and the useful life of houses can be extended by building with the best and most permanent materials available. The best and most permanent materials in many cases are, however, much more expensive than materials which require more maintenance. The most economical procedure in home building has been to compromise between the capital costs of high quality and enduring materials and the maintenance costs of less desirable materials. 24.____
On the basis of this statement, one would be justified in stating that:

A. Savings in maintenance costs make the use of less durable and less expensive building materials preferable to high quality materials that would prolong the useful life of houses constructed from them
B. Financial advantage can be secured by the home builder if he judiciously combines costly but enduring building materials with less desirable materials which, however, require more maintenance
C. A compromise between the capital costs of high quality materials and the maintenance costs of less desirable materials makes it easier for a home builder to estimate construction expenditures
D. The most economical procedure in home building is to balance the capital costs of the most permanent materials against the costs of less expensive materials that are cheaper to maintain

25. Personnel selection has been a critical problem for local housing authorities. The pool of qualified workers trained in housing procedures is small, and the colleges and universities have failed to grasp the opportunity for enlarging it. While real estate experience makes a good background for management of a housing project, many real estate men are deplorably lacking in understanding of social and governmental problems. Social workers, on the other hand, are likely to be deficient in business judgment. 25.____
On the basis of this statement, it would be MOST accurate to state that:

A. Colleges and universities have failed to train qualified workers for proficiency in housing procedures
B. Social workers are deficient in business judgment as related to the management of a housing project
C. Real estate experience makes a person a good manager of a housing project
D. Local housing authorities have been critical of present methods of personnel selection

KEY (CORRECT ANSWERS)

1. B
2. C
3. B
4. B
5. D
6. B
7. B
8. D
9. D
10. D
11. A
12. D
13. A
14. D
15. A
16. A
17. B
18. C
19. A
20. C
21. B
22. B
23. C
24. B
25. A

PREPARING WRITTEN MATERIAL

PARAGRAPH REARRANGEMENT COMMENTARY

The sentences that follow are in scrambled order. You are to rearrange them in proper order and indicate the letter choice containing the correct answer at the space at the right.

Each group of sentences in this section is actually a paragraph presented in scrambled order. Each sentence in the group has a place in that paragraph; no sentence is to be left out. You are to read each group of sentences and decide upon the best order in which to put the sentences so as to form a well-organized paragraph.

The questions in this section measure the ability to solve a problem when all the facts relevant to its solution are not given.

More specifically, certain positions of responsibility and authority require the employee to discover connection between events sometimes, apparently, unrelated. In order to do this, the employee will find it necessary to correctly infer that unspecified events have probably occurred or are likely to occur. This ability becomes especially important when action must be taken on incomplete information.

Accordingly, these questions require competitors to choose among several suggested alternatives, each of which presents a different sequential arrangement of the events. Competitors must choose the MOST logical of the suggested sequences.

In order to do so, they may be required to draw on general knowledge to infer missing concepts or events that are essential to sequencing the given events. Competitors should be careful to infer only what is essential to the sequence. The plausibility of the wrong alternatives will always require the inclusion of unlikely events or of additional chains of events which are NOT essential to sequencing the given events.

It's very important to remember that you are looking for the best of the four possible choices, and that the best choice of all may not even be one of the answers you're given to choose from.

There is no one right way to solve these problems. Many people have found it helpful to first write out the order of the sentences, as they would have arranged them, on their scrap paper before looking at the possible answers. If their optimum answer is there, this can save them some time. If it isn't, this method can still give insight into solving the problem. Others find it most helpful to just go through each of the possible choices, contrasting each as they go along. You should use whatever method feels comfortable and works for you.

While most of these types of questions are not that difficult, we've added a higher percentage of the difficult type, just to give you more practice. Usually there are only one or two questions on this section that contain such subtle distinctions that you're unable to answer confidently. And you then may find yourself stuck deciding between two possible choices, neither of which you're sure about.

PREPARING WRITTEN MATERIAL

PARAGRAPH REARRANGEMENT COMMENTARY

EXAMINATION SECTION

TEST 1

DIRECTIONS: The sentences that follow are in scrambled order. You are to rearrange them in proper order and indicate the letter choice containing the correct answer. *PRINT THE LETTER OF THE CORRECT ANSWER IN THE SPACE AT THE RIGHT.*

1. Below are four statements labeled W, X, Y and Z. 1.____
   W. He was a strict and fanatic drillmaster.
   X. The word is always used in a derogatory sense and generally shows resentment and anger on the part of the user.
   Y. It is from the name of this Frenchman that we derive our English word, martinet.
   Z. Jean Martinet was the Inspector-General of Infantry during the reign of King Louis XIV.

   The PROPER order in which these sentences should be placed in a paragraph is:
   A. X, Z, W, Y B. X, Z, Y, W C. Z, W, Y, X D. Z, Y, W, X

2. In the following paragraph, the sentences, which are numbered, have been jumbled. 2.____
   I. Since then it has undergone changes.
   II. It was incorporated in 1955 under the laws of the State of New York.
   III. Its primary purposes, a cleaner city, has, however, remained the same.
   IV. The Citizens Committee works in cooperation with the Mayor's Inter-departmental Committee for a Clean City. 3.____

   The order in which these sentences should be arranged to form a well-organized paragraph is:
   A. II, IV, I, III B. III, IV, I, II C. IV, II, I, III D. IV, III, II, I

Questions 3-5.

DIRECTIONS: The sentences listed below are part of a meaningful paragraph but they are not given in their proper order. You are to decide what would be the BEST order in which to put the sentences so as to form a well-organized paragraph. Each sentence has a place in the paragraph; there are no extra sentences. You are then to answer Questions 3 through 5 inclusive on the basis of your rearrangements of these scrambled sentences into a properly organized paragraph.

In 1887 some insurance companies organized an Inspection Department to advise their clients on all phases of fire prevention and protection. Probably this has been due to the smaller annual fire losses in Great Britain than in the United States. It tests various fire prevention devices and appliances and determines manufacturing hazards and their safeguards. Fire research began earlier in the United States and is more advanced than in Great Britain. Later they established a laboratory specializing in electrical, mechanical, hydraulic, and chemical fields.

3. When the five sentences are arranged in proper order, the paragraph starts with the sentence which begins 3.____
   A. "In 1887..." B. "Probably this..." C. "It tests..."
   D. "Fire research..." E. "Later they..."

4. In the last sentence listed above, "they" refers to 4.____
   A. the insurance companies
   B. the United States and Great Britain
   C. the Inspection Department
   D. clients
   E. technicians

5. When the above paragraph is properly arranged, it ends with the words 5.____
   A. "...and protection."
   B. "...the United States."
   C. "...their safeguards."
   D. "...in Great Britain."
   E. "...chemical fields."

KEY (CORRECT ANSWERS)

1. C
2. C
3. D
4. A
5. C

TEST 2

DIRECTIONS: In each of the questions numbered I through V, several sentences are given. For each question, choose as your answer the group of number that represents the MOST logical order of these sentences if they were arranged in paragraph form. *PRINT THE LETTER OF THE CORRECT ANSWER IN THE SPACE AT THE RIGHT.*

1. I. It is established when one shows that the landlord has prevented the tenant's enjoyment of his interest in the property leased. 1.____
   II. Constructive eviction is the result of a breach of the covenant of quiet enjoyment implied in all leases.
   III. In some parts of the United States, it is not complete until the tenant vacates within a reasonable time.
   IV. Generally, the acts must be of such serious and permanent character as to deny the tenant the enjoyment of his possessing rights.
   V. In this event, upon abandonment of the premises, the tenant's liability for that ceases.

   The CORRECT answer is:
   A. II, I, IV, III, V
   B. V, II, III, I, IV
   C. IV, III, I, II, V
   D. I, III, V, IV, II

2. I. The powerlessness before private and public authorities that is the typical experience of the slum tenant is reminiscent of the situation of blue-collar workers all through the nineteenth century. 2.____
   II. Similarly, in recent years, this chapter of history has been reopened by anti-poverty groups which have attempted to organize slum tenants to enable them to bargain collectively with their landlords about the conditions of their tenancies.
   III. It is familiar history that many of the worker remedied their condition by joining together and presenting their demands collectively.
   IV. Like the workers, tenants are forced by the conditions of modern life into substantial dependence on these who possess great political aid and economic power.
   V. What's more, the very fact of dependence coupled with an absence of education and self-confidence makes them hesitant and unable to stand up for what they need from those in power.

   The CORRECT answer is:
   A. V, IV, I, II, III
   B. II, III, I, V, IV
   C. III, I, V, IV, II
   D. I, IV, V, III, II

3. I. A railroad, for example, when not acting as a common carrier may contract away responsibility for its own negligence. 3.____
   II. As to a landlord, however, no decision has been found relating to the legal effect of a clause shifting the statutory duty of repair to the tenant.
   III. The courts have not passed on the validity of clauses relieving the landlord of this duty and liability.
   IV. They have, however, upheld the validity of exculpatory clauses in other types of contracts.

V. Housing regulations impose a duty upon the landlord to maintain leased premises in safe condition.
VI. As another example, a bailee may limit his liability except for gross negligence, willful acts, or fraud.

The CORRECT answer is:
A. II, I, VI, IV, III, V
B. I, III, IV, V, VI, II
C. III, V, I, IV, II, VI
D. V, III, IV, I, VI, II

4. I. Since there are only samples in the building, retail or consumer sales are generally eschewed by mart occupants, and in some instances, rigid controls are maintained to limit entrance to the mart only to those persons engaged in retailing. 4.____
II. Since World War I, in many larger cities, there has developed a new type of property, called the mart building.
III. It can, therefore, be used by wholesalers and jobbers for the display of sample merchandise.
IV. This type of building is most frequently a multi-storied, finished interior property which is a cross between a retail arcade and a loft building.
V. This limitation enables the mart occupants to ship the orders from another location after the retailer or dealer makes his selection from the samples.

The CORRECT answer is:
A. II, IV, III, I, V
B. IV, III, V, I, II
C. I, III, II, IV, V
D. I, IV, II, III, V

5. I. In general, staff-line friction reduces the distinctive contribution of staff personnel. 5.____
II. The conflicts, however, introduce an uncontrolled element into the managerial system.
III. On the other hand, the natural resistance of the line to staff innovations probably usefully restrains over-eager efforts to apply untested procedures on a large scale.
IV. Under such conditions, it is difficult to know when valuable ideas are being sacrificed.
V. The relatively weak position of staff, requiring accommodation to the line, tends to restrict their ability to engage in free, experimental innovation.

The CORRECT answer is:
A. IV, II, III, I, V
B. I, V, III, II, IV
C. V, III, I, II, IV
D. II, I, IV, V, III

KEY (CORRECT ANSWERS)

1. A
2. D
3. D
4. A
5. B

TEST 3

DIRECTIONS: Questions 1 through 4 consist of six sentences which can be arranged in a logical sequence. For each question, select the choice which places the numbered sentences in the MOST logical sequent. *PRINT THE LETTER OF THE CORRECT ANSWER IN THE SPACE AT THE RIGHT.*

1. I. The burden of proof as to each issue is determined before trial and remains upon the same party throughout the trial. 1.____
   II. The jury is at liberty to believe one witness' testimony as against a number of contradictory witnesses.
   III. In a civil case, the party bearing the burden of proof is required to prove his contention by a fair preponderance of the evidence.
   IV. However, it must be noted that a fair preponderance of evidence does not necessarily mean a greater number of witnesses.
   V. The burden of proof is the burden which rests upon one of the parties to an action to persuade the trier of the facts, generally the jury, that a proposition he asserts is true.
   VI. If the evidence is equally balanced, or if it leaves the jury in such doubt as to be unable to decide the controversy either way, judgment must be given against the party upon whom the burden of proof rests.

   The CORRECT answer is:
   A. III, II, V, IV, I, VI
   B. I, II, VI, V, III, IV
   C. III, IV, V, I, II, VI
   D. V, I, III, VI, IV, II

2. I. If a parent is without assets and is unemployed, he cannot be convicted of the crime of non-support of a child. 2.____
   II. The term "sufficient ability" has been held to mean sufficient financial ability.
   III. It does not matter if his unemployment is by choice or unavoidable circumstances.
   IV. If he fails to take any steps at all, he may be liable to prosecution for endangering the welfare of a child.
   V. Under the penal law, a parent is responsible for the support of his minor child only if the parent is "of sufficient ability."
   VI. An indigent parent may meet his obligation by borrowing money or by seeking aid under the provisions of the Social Welfare Law.

   The CORRECT answer is:
   A. VI, I, V, III, II, IV
   B. I, III, V, II, IV, VI
   C. V, II, I, III, VI, IV
   D. I, VI, IV, V, II, III

3. I. Consider, for example, the case of a rabble rouser who urges a group of twenty people to go out and break the windows of a nearby factory. 3.____
   II. Therefore, the law fills the indicated gap with the crime of inciting to riot.
   III. A person is considered guilty of inciting to riot when he urges ten or more persons to engage in tumultuous and violent conduct of a kind likely to create public alarm.
   IV. However, if he has not obtained the cooperation of at least four people, he cannot be charged with unlawful assembly.

V. The charge of inciting to riot was added to the law to cover types of conduct which cannot be classified as either the crime of "riot" or the crime of "unlawful assembly."
VI. If he acquires the acquiescence of at least four of them, he is guilty of unlawful assembly even if the project does not materialize.

The CORRECT answer is:
A. III, V, I, VI, IV, II
B. V, I, IV, VI, II, III
C. III, IV, I, V, II, VI
D. V, I, IV, VI, III, II

4. I. If, however, the rebuttal evidence presents an issue of credibility, it is for the jury to determine whether the presumption has, in fact, been destroyed. 4.____
II. Once sufficient evidence to the contrary is introduced, the presumption disappears from the trial.
III. The effect of a presumption is to place the burden upon the adversary to come forward with evidence to rebut the presumption.
IV. When a presumption is overcome and ceases to exist in the case, the fact or facts which gave rise to the presumption still remain.
V. Whether a presumption has been overcome is ordinarily a question for the court.
VI. Such information may furnish a basis for a logical inference.

The CORRECT answer is:
A. IV, VI, II, V, I, III
B. III, II, V, I, IV, VI
C. V, III, VI, IV, II, I
D. V, IV, I, II, VI, III

KEY (CORRECT ANSWERS)

1. D
2. C
3. A
4. B

PREPARING WRITTEN MATERIAL
PARAGRAPH REARRANGEMENT

EXAMINATION SECTION

TEST 1

DIRECTIONS: The following groups of sentences need to be arranged in an order that makes sense. Select the letter preceding the sequence that represents the best sentence order. *PRINT THE LETTER OF THE CORRECT ANSWER IN THE SPACE AT THE RIGHT.*

1. I. The ostrich egg shell's legendary toughness makes it an excellent substitute for certain types of dishes or dinnerware, and in parts of Africa ostrich shells are cut and decorated for use as containers for water. 1.____
   II. Since prehistoric times, people have used the enormous egg of the ostrich as a part of their diet, a practice which has required much patience and hard work—to hard boil an ostrich egg takes about four hours.
   III. Opening the egg's shell, which is rock hard and nearly an inch thick, requires heavy tools, such as a saw or chisel; from inside, a baby ostrich must use a hornlike projection on its beak as a miniature pick-axe to escape from the egg.
   IV. The offspring of all higher-order animals originate from single egg cells that are carried by mothers, and most of these eggs are relatively small, often microscopic.
   V. The egg of the African ostrich, however, weighs a massive thirty pounds, making it the largest single cell on earth, and a common object of human curiosity and wonder.

   The BEST order is:
   A. V, IV, I, II, III B. I, IV, V, III, II C. IV, II, III, V, I D. IV, V, II, III, I

2. I. Typically only a few feet high on the open sea, individual tsunami have been known to circle the entire globe two or three times if their progress is not interrupted, but are not usually dangerous until they approach the shallow water that surrounds land masses. 2.____
   II. Some of the most terrifying and damaging hazards caused by earthquakes are tsunami, which were once called "tidal waves"—a poorly chosen name, since these waves have nothing to do with tides.
   III Then a wave, slowed by the sudden drag on the lower part of its moving water column, will pile upon itself, sometimes reaching a height of over 100 feet.
   IV. Tsunami (Japanese for "great harbor wave") are seismic waves that are caused by earthquakes near oceanic trenches, and once triggered, can travel up to 600 miles an hour on the open ocean.
   V. A land-shoaling tsunami is capable of extraordinary destruction; some tsunami have deposited large boats miles inland, washed out two-foot-thick seawalls, and scattered locomotive trains over long distances.

   The BEST order is:
   A. IV, I, III, II, V B. I, III, IV, II, V C. V, I, III, II, IV D. II, IV, I, III, V

3. I. Soon, by the 1940s, jazz was the most popular type of music among American intellectuals and college students. 3.____
II. In the early days of jazz, it was considered "lowdown" music, or music that was played only in rough, disreputable bars and taverns.
III. However, jazz didn't take too long to develop from early ragtime melodies into more complex, sophisticated forms, such as Charlie Parker's "bebop" style of jazz.
IV. After charismatic band leaders such as Duke Ellington and Count Basie brought jazz to a larger audience, and jazz continued to evolve into more complicated forms, white audiences began to accept and even to enjoy the new American art form.
V. Many white Americans, who then dictated the tastes of society, were wary of music that was played almost exclusively in black clubs in the poorer sections of cities and towns.
The BEST order is:
A. V, IV, III, II, I B. II, V, III, IV, I C. IV, V, III, I, II D. I, II, IV, III, V

4. I. Then, hanging in a windless place, the magnetized end of the needle would always point to the south. 4.____
II. The needle could then be balanced on the rim of a cup, or the edge of a fingernail, but this balancing act was hard to maintain, and the needle often fell off.
III. Other needles would point to the north, and it was important for any traveler finding his way with a compass to remember which kind of magnetized needle he was carrying.
IV. To make some of the earliest compasses in recorded history, ancient Chinese "magicians" would rub a needle with a piece of magnetized iron called a lodestone.
V. A more effective method of keeping the needle free to swing with its magnetic pull was to attach a strand of silk to the center of the needle with a tiny piece of wax.
The BEST order is:
A. IV, II, V, I, III B. IV, III, V, II, I C. IV, V, II, I, III D. IV, I, III, V, II

5. I The now-famous first mate of the *H.M.S. Bounty*, Fletcher Christian, founded one of the world's most peculiar civilizations in 1790. 5.____
II. The men knew they had just committed a crime for which they could be hanged, so they set sail for Pitcairn, a remote, abandoned island in the far eastern region of the Polynesian archipelago, accompanied by twelve Polynesian women and six men.
III. In a mutiny that has become legendary, Christian and the others forced Captain Bligh into a lifeboat and set him adrift off the coast of Tonga in April of 1789.
IV. In early 1790, the *Bounty* landed at Pitcairn Island, where the men lived out the rest of their lives and founded an isolated community which to this day includes direct descendants of Christian and the other Crewmen.

V. The *Bounty*, commanded by Captain William Bligh, was in the middle of a global voyage, and Christian and his shipmates had come to the conclusion that Bligh was a reckless madman who would lead them to their deaths unless they took the ship from him.

The BEST order is:

A. IV, V, III, II, I B. I, III, V, II, IV C. I, V, III, II, IV D. III, I, V, IV, II

6. I. But once the vines had been led to make orchids, the flowers had to be carefully hand-pollinated, because unpollinated orchids usually lasted less than a day, wilting and dropping off the vine before it had even become dark. 6.____

II. The Totonac farmers discovered that looping a vine back around once it reached a five-foot height on its host tree would cause the vine to flower.

III. Though they knew how to process the fruit pods and extract vanilla's flavoring agent, the Totonacs also knew that a wild vanilla vine did not produce abundant flowers or fruit.

IV. Wild vines climbed along the trunks and canopies of trees, and this constant upward growth diverted most of the vine's energy to making leaves instead of the orchid flowers that once pollinated, would produce the flavorful pods.

V. Hundreds of years before vanilla became a prized food flavoring in Europe and the Western World, the Totonac Indians of the Mexican Gulf Coast were skilled cultivators of the vanilla vine, whose fruit they literally worshipped as a goddess.

The BEST order is:

A. II, III, IV, I, V B. II, IV, III, I, V C. V, III, IV, II, I D. III, IV, I, II, V

7. I. Once airborne, the spider is at the mercy of the air currents—usually the spider takes a brief journey, traveling close to the ground, but some have been found in air samples collected as high as 10,000 feet, or been reported landing on ships far out at sea. 7.____

II. Once a young spider has hatched, it must leave the environment into which it was born as quickly as possible, in order to avoid competing with its hundreds of brothers and sisters for food.

III. The silk rises into warm air currents, and as soon as the pull feels adequate the spider lets go and drifts up into the air, suspended from the silk strand in the same way that a person might parasail.

IV. To help young spiders do this, many species have adapted a practice known as "aerial dispersal," or, in common speech, "ballooning."

V. A spider that wants to leave its surroundings quickly will climb to the top of a grass system or twig, face into the wind, and aim its back end into the air, releasing a long stream of silk from the glands near the tip of its abdomen.

The BEST order is:

A. V, IV, II, III, I B. V, II, IV, I, III C. II, V, IV, III, I D. II, IV, V, III, I

8. I. For about a year, Tycho worked at a castle in Prague with a scientist named Johannes Kepler, but their association was cut short by another argument that drove Kepler out of the castle, to later develop, on his own, the theory of planetary orbits. 8.____
   II. Tycho found life without a nose embarrassing, so he made a new nose for himself out of silver, which reportedly remained glued to his face for the rest of his life.
   III. Tycho Brahe, the 17th-century Danish astronomer, is today more famous for his odd and arrogant personality than for any contribution he has made to our knowledge of the stars and planets.
   IV. Early in his career, as a student at Rostock University, Tycho got into an argument with another student about who was the better mathematician, and the two became so angry that the argument turned into a sword fight, during which Tycho's nose was sliced off.
   V. Later in his life, Tycho's arrogance may have kept him from playing a part in one of the greatest astronomical discoveries in history: the elliptical orbits of the solar system's planets.

   The BEST order is:
   A. I, IV, II, III, V B. IV, II, III, V, I C. IV, II, I, III, V D. III, IV, II, V, I

9. I. The processionaries are so used to this routine that if a person picks up the end of a silk line and brings it back to the origin—creating a closed circle—the caterpillars may travel around and around for days, sometimes starving or freezing, without changing course. 9.____
   II. Rather than relying on sight or sound, the other caterpillars, who are lined up end-to-end behind the leader, travel to and from their nests by walking on this silk line, and each will reinforce it by laying down its own marking line as it passes over.
   III. In order to insure the safety of individuals, the processionary caterpillar nests in a tree with dozens of other caterpillars, and at night, when it is safest, they all leave together in search of food.
   IV. The processionary caterpillar of the European continent is a perfect illustration of how much some inspect species rely on instinct in their daily routines.
   V. As they leave their nests, the processionaries form a single-file line behind a leader who spins and lays out a silk line to mark the chosen path.

   The BEST order is:
   A. IV, III, V, II, I B. III, V, IV, II, I C. III, V, II, I, IV D. IV, V, III, I, II

10. I. Often, the child is also given a handcrafted walker or push cart, to provide support for its first upright explorations. 10.____
   II. In traditional Indian families, a child's first steps are celebrated as a ceremonial event, rooted in ancient myth.
   III. These carts are often intricately designed to resemble the chariot of Krishna, an important figure in Indian mythology.
   IV. The sound of these anklet bells is intended to mimic the footsteps of the legendary child Rama, who is celebrated in devotional songs throughout India.

V. When the child's parents see that the child is ready to begin walking, they will fit it with specially designed ankle bracelets, adorned with gently ringing bells.

The BEST order is:

A. II, III, IV, I, V B. II, V, III, I, IV C. V, IV, I, III, II D. V, III, II, I, IV

11. I. The settlers planted Osage oranges all across Middle America, and today long lines and rectangles of Osage orange trees can still be seen on the prairies, running along the former boundaries of farms that no longer exist. 11.____

II. After trying sod walls and water-filled ditches with no success, American farmers began to look for a plant that was adaptable to prairie weather, and that could be trimmed into a hedge that was "pig-tight, horse-high, and bull-strong."

III. The tree, so named because it bore a large (but inedible) fruit the size of an orange, was among the sturdiest and hardiest of American trees, and was prized among Native Americans for the strength and flexibility of bows which were made from its wood.

IV. The first people to practice agriculture on the American flatlands were faced with an important problem: what would they use to fence their land in a place that was almost entirely without trees or rocks?

V. Finally, an Illinois farmer brought the settlers a tree that was native to the land between the Red and Arkansas rivers, a tree called the Osage orange.

The BEST order is:

A. II, I, V, III, IV B. I, II, III, IV, V C. IV, II, V, III, I D. IV, II, I, III, V

12. I. After about ten minutes of such spirited and complicated activity, the head dancer is free to make up his or her own movements while maintaining the interest of the New Year's crowd. 12.____

II. The dancer will then perform a series of leg kicks, while at the same time operating the lion's mouth with his own hand and moving the ears and eyes by means of a string which is attached to the dancer's own mouth.

III. The most difficult role of this dance belongs to the one who controls the lion's head; this person must lead all the other "parts" of the lion through the choreographed segments of the dance.

IV. The head dancer begins with a complex series of steps. alternately stepping forward with the head raised, and then retreating a few steps while lowering the head, a movement that is intended to create the impression that the lion is keeping a watchful eye for anything evil.

V. When performing a traditional Chinese New Year's lion dance, several performers must fit themselves inside a large lion costume and work together to enact different parts of the dance.

The BEST order is:

A. V, III, IV, II, I B. III, IV, II, V, I C. III, I, V, IV, II D. IV, II, III, V, I

13. I. For many years the shell of the chambered nautilus was treasured in Europe for its beauty and intricacy, but collectors were unaware that they were in possession of the structure that marked a "missing link" in the evolution of marine mollusks. 13.____
   II. The nautilus, however, evolved a series of enclosed chambers in its shell, and invented a new use for the structure: the shell began to serve as a buoyancy device.
   III. Equipped with this new flotation device, the nautilus did not need the single, muscular foot of its predecessors, but instead developed flaps, tentacles, and a gentle form of jet propulsion that transformed it into the first mollusk able to take command of its own density and explore a three-dimensional world.
   IV. By pumping and adjusting air pressure into the chambers, the nautilus could spend the day resting on the bottom, and then rise toward the surface at night in search of food.
   V. The nautilus shell looks like a large snail shell, similar to those of its ancestors, who used their shells as protective coverings while they were anchored to the sea floor.

   The BEST order is:
   A. V, II, IV, I, III B. V, I, II, III, IV C. I, II, V, III, IV D. I, V, II, IV, III

14. I. While France and England battled for control of the region, the Acadiens prospered on the fertile farmland, which was finally secured by England in 1713. 14.____
   II. Early in the 17th century, settlers from Western France founded a colony called Acadie in what is now the Canadian province of Nova Scotia.
   III. At this time, English officials feared the presence of spies among the Acadiens who might be loyal to their French homeland, and the Acadiens were deported to spots along the Atlantic and Caribbean shores of America.
   IV. The French settlers remained on this land, under English rule, for around forty years, until the beginning of the French and Indian War, another conflict between France and England.
   V. As the Acadien refugees drifted toward a final home in Southern Louisiana, neighbors shortened their name to "Cadien," and finally "Cajun," the name which the descendants of early Acadiens still call themselves.

   The BEST order is:
   A. I, IV, II, III, V B. II, I, III, V, IV C. II, I, IV, III, V D. V, II, III, IV, I

15. I. Traditional households in the Eastern and Western regions of Africa serve two meals a day—one at around noon, and the other in the evening. 15.____
   II. The starch is then used in the way that Americans might use a spoon, to scoop up a portion of the main dish on the person's plate.
   III. The reason for the starch's inclusion in every meal has to do with taste as well as nutrition; African food can be very spicy, and the starch is known to cool the burning effect of the main dish.
   IV. When serving these meals, the main dish is usually served on individual plates, and the starch is served on a communal plate, from which diners break off a piece of bread or scoop rice or fufu in their fingers.

V. The typical meals usually consist of a thick stew or soup as the main course, and an accompanying starch—either bread, rice, or *fufu*, a starchy grain paste similar in consistency to mashed potatoes.

The BEST order is:

A. V, II, III, IV, I B. V, I, IV, III, II C. I, IV, V, III, II D. I, V, IV, II, III

16. I. In the early days of the American Midwest, Indiana settlers sometimes came together to hold an event called an apple peeling, where neighboring settlers gathered at the homestead of a host family to help prepare the hosts' apple crop for cooking, canning, and making apple butter. 16.____

II. At the beginning of the event, each peeler sat down in front of a ten- or twenty-gallon stone jar and was given a crock of apples and a paring knife.

III. Once a peeler had finished with a crock, another was placed next to him; if the peeler was an unmarried man, he kept a strict count of the number of apples he had peeled, because the winner was allowed to kiss the girl of his choice.

IV. The peeling usually ended by 9:30 in the evening, when the neighbors gathered in the host family's parlor for a dance social.

V. The apples were peeled, cored, and quartered, and then placed into the jar.

The BEST order is:

A. I, V, III, IV, II B. II, V, III, IV, I C. I, II, V, III, IV D. II, I, V, IV, III

17. I. If your pet turtle is a land turtle and is native to temperate climates, it will stop eating some time in October, which should be your cue to prepare the turtle for hibernation. 17.____

II. The box should then be covered with a wire screen, which will protect the turtle from any rodents or predators that might want to take advantage of a motionless and helpless animal.

III. When your turtle hasn't eaten for a while and appears ready to hibernate, it should be moved to its winter quarters, most likely a cellar or garage, where the temperature should range between 40° and 45°F.

IV. Instead of feeding the turtle, you should bathe it every day in warm water, to encourage the turtle to empty its intestines in preparation for its long winter sleep.

V. Here the turtle should be placed in a well-ventilated box whose bottom is covered with a moisture-absorbing layer of clay beads, and then filled three-fourths full with almost dry peat moss or wood chips, into which the turtle will burrow and sleep for several months.

The BEST order is:

A. I, IV, III, V, II B. III, IV, II, V, I C. III, II, IV, I, V D. IV, V, II, III, I

18. I. Once he has reached the nest, the hunter uses two sturdy bamboo poles like huge chopsticks to pull the next away from the mountainside, into a large basket that will be lowered to people waiting below. 18.____

II. The world's largest honeybees colonize the Nealese mountainsides, building honeycombs as large as a person on sheer rock faces that are often hundreds of feet high.

III. In the remote mountain country of Nepal, a small band of "honey hunters" carry out a tradition so ancient that 10,000 year-old drawings of the practice have been found in the caves of Nepal.
IV. To harvest the honey and beeswax from these combs, a honey hunter climbs above the nests, lowers a long bamboo-fiber ladder over the cliff, and then climbs down.
V. Throughout this dangerous practice, the hunter is stung repeatedly, and only the veterans, with skin that has been toughened over the years, are able to return from a hunt without the painful swelling caused by stings.

The BEST order is:
A. II, IV, III, V, I B. II, IV, I, V, III C. V, III, II, IV, I D. III, II, IV, I, V

19. I. After the Romans left Britain, there were relentless attacks on the islands from the barbarian tribes of northern Germany—the Angles, Saxons, and Jutes. 19.____
II. As the empire weakened, Roman soldiers withdrew from Britain, leaving behind a country that continued to practice the Christian religion that had been introduced by the Romans.
III. Early Latin writings tell of a Christian warrior named Arturius (Arthur, in English) who led the British citizens to defeat these barbarian invades, and brought an extended period of peace to the lands of Britain.
IV. Long ago, the British Isles were part of the far-flung Roman Empire that extended across most of Europe and into Africa and Asia.
V. The romantic legend of King Arthur and his knights of the Round Table, one of the most popular and widespread stories of all time, appears to have some foundation in history.

The BEST order is:
A. V, IV, III, II, I B. V, IV, II, I, III C. IV, V, II, III, I D. IV, III, II, I, V

20. I. The cylinder was allowed to cool until it could stand on its own, and then it was cut from the tube and split down the side with a single straight cut. 20.____
II. Nineteenth-century glassmakers, who had not yet discovered the glazier's modern techniques for making panes of glass, had to create a method for converting their blown gas into flat sheets.
III. The bubble was then pierced at the end to make a hole that opened up while the glassmaker gently spun it, creating a cylinder of glass.
IV. Turned on its side and laid on a conveyor belt, the cylinder was strengthened, or tempered, by being heated again and cooled very slowly, eventually flattening out into a single rectangular of glass.
V. To do this, the glassmaker dipped the end of a long tube into melted glass and blew into the other end of the tube, creating an expanding bubble of glass.

The BEST order is:
A. II, V, III, IV, I B. II, IV, V, III, I C. III, V, II, IV, I D. III, I, IV, V, II

21. I. The splints are almost always hidden, but horses are occasionally born whose splinted toes project from the leg on either side, just above the hoof. 21.____
    II. The second and fourth toes remained, but shrank to thin splints of bone that fused invisibly to the horse's leg bone.
    III. Horses are unique among mammals, having evolved feet that each end in what is essentially a single toe, capped by a large, sturdy hoof.
    IV. Julius Caesar, an emperor of ancient Rome, was said to have owned one of these three-toed horses, and considered it so special that he would not permit anyone else to ride it.
    V. Though the horse's earlier ancestors possessed the traditional mammalian set of five toes on each foot, the horse has retained only its third toe; its first and fifth toes disappeared completely as the horse evolved.

    The BEST order is:
    A. III, V, II, I, IV B. V, III, II, IV, I C. III, II, V, I, IV D. V, II, III, I, IV

22. I. The new building materials—some of which are twenty feet long, and weigh nearly six tons—were transported to Pohnpei on rafts, and were brought into their present position by using hibiscus fiber ropes and leverage to move the stone columns upward along the inclined trunks of coconut palm trees. 22.____
    II. The ancestors built great fires to heat the stone, and then poured cool seawater on the columns, which caused the stone to contract and split along natural fracture lines.
    III. The now-abandoned enclave of Nan Madol, a group of 92 man-made islands off the shore of the Micronesian island of Pohnpei, is estimated to have been built around the year 500 A.D.
    IV. The islanders say their ancestors quarried stone columns from a nearby island, where large basalt columns were formed by the cooling of molten lava.
    V. The structures of Nan Madol are remarkable for the sheer size of some of the stone "longs" or columns that were used to create the walls of the offshore community, and today anthropologists can only rely on the information of existing local people for clues about how Nan Madol was built.

    The BEST order is:
    A. V, IV, III, II, I B. V, III, I, IV, II C. III, V, IV, II, I D. III, I, IV, II, V

23. I. One of the most easily manipulated substances on earth, glass can be made into ceramic tiles that are composed of over 90% air. 22.____
    II. NASA's space shuttles are the first spacecraft ever designed to leave and re-enter the earth's atmosphere while remaining intact.
    III. These ceramic tiles are such effective insulators that when a tile emerges from the oven in which it was fired, it can be held safely in a person's hand by the edges while its interior still glows at a temperature well over 2000°F.
    IV. Eventually, the engineers were led to a material that is as old as our most ancient civilization.
    V. Because the temperature during atmospheric re-entry is so incredibly hot, it took NASA's engineers some time to find a substance capable of protecting the shuttles.

The BEST order is:
A. V, II, I, II, IV B. II, V, IV, I, III C. II, III, I, IV, V D. V, IV, III, I, II

24. I. The secret to teaching any parakeet to talk is patience, and the understanding that when a bird talks," it is simply imitating what it hears, rather than putting ideas into words. 24.____
II. You should stay just out of sight of the bird and repeat the phrase you want it to learn, for at least fifteen minutes every morning and evening.
III. It is important to leave the bird without any words of encouragement or farewell; otherwise it might combine stray remarks or phrases, such as "Good night," with the phrase you are trying to teach it.
IV. For this reason, to train your bird to imitate your words you should keep it free of any distractions, especially other noises, while you are giving it "lesson."
V. After your repetition, you should quietly leave the bird alone for a while, to think over what it has just heard.
The BEST order is:
A. I, IV, II, V, III B. I, II, IV, III, V C. III, II, I, V, IV D. III, I, V, IV, II

25. I. As a school approaches, fishermen from neighboring communities join their fishing boats together as a fleet, and string their gill nets together to make a huge fence that is held up by cork floats. 25.____
II. At a signal from the party leaders, or *nakura*, the family members pound the sides of the boats or beat the water with long poles, creating a sudden and deafening noise.
III. The fishermen work together to drag the trap into a half-circle that may reach 300 yards in diameter, and then the families move their boats to form the other half of the circle around the school of fish.
IV. The school of fish flee from the commotion into the awaiting trap, where a final wall of net is thrown over the open end of the half-circle, securing the day's haul.
V. Indonesian people from the area around the Sulu islands live on the sea, in floating villages made of lashed-together or stilted homes, and make much of their living by fishing their home waters for migrating schools of snapper, scad, and other fish.
The BEST order is:
A. I, V, III, IV, II B. I, II, IV, III, V C. V, I, II, III, IV D. V, I, III, II, IV

KEY (CORRECT ANSWERS)

1.	D	11.	C
2.	D	12.	A
3.	B	13.	D
4.	A	14.	C
5.	C	15.	D
6.	C	16.	C
7.	D	17.	A
8.	D	18.	D
9.	A	19.	B
10.	B	20.	A

21.	A
22.	C
23.	B
24.	A
25.	D

PREPARING WRITTEN MATERIAL

EXAMINATION SECTION

TEST 1

DIRECTIONS: Each question consists of a sentence which may or may not be an example of good English usage. Examine each sentence, considering grammar, punctuation, spelling, capitalization, and awkwardness. Then choose the correct statement about it from the four choices below it. If the English usage in the sentence given is better than any of the changes suggested in choices B, C, or D, pick choice A. (Do not pick a choice that will change the meaning of the sentence.) *PRINT THE LETTER OF THE CORRECT ANSWER IN THE SPACE AT THE RIGHT.*

1. We attended a staff conference on Wednesday the new safety and fire rules were discussed. 1.____
   A. This is an example of acceptable writing.
   B. The words "safety," "fire," and "rules" should begin with capital letters.
   C. There should be a comma after the word "Wednesday."
   D. There should be a period after the word "Wednesday" and the word "the" should begin with a capital letter.

2. Neither the dictionary or the telephone directory could be found in the office library. 2.____
   A. This is an example of acceptable writing.
   B. The word "or" should be changed to "nor."
   C. The word "library" should be spelled "libery."
   D. The word "neither" should be changed to "either."

3. The report would have been typed correctly if the typist could read the draft. 3.____
   A. This is an example of acceptable writing.
   B. The word "would" should be removed.
   C. The word "have" should be inserted after the word "could."
   D. The word "correctly" should be changed to "correct."

4. The supervisor brought the reports and forms to an employees desk. 4.____
   A. This is an example of acceptable writing.
   B. The word "brought" should be changed to "took."
   C. There should be a comma after the word "reports" and a comma after the word "forms."
   D. The word "employees" should be spelled "employee's."

5. It's important for all the office personnel to submit their vacation schedules on time. 5.____
   A. This is an example of acceptable writing.
   B. The word "It's" should be spelled "Its."
   C. The word "their" should be spelled "they're."
   D. The word "personnel" should be spelled "personal."

6. The report, along with the accompanying documents, were submitted for review. 6.____
   A. This is an example of acceptable writing.
   B. The words "were submitted" should be changed to "was submitted."
   C. The word "accompanying" should be spelled "accompaning."
   D. The comma after the word "report" should be taken out.

7. If others must use your files, be certain that they understand how the system works, but insist that you do all the filing and refiling. 7.____
   A. This is an example of acceptable writing.
   B. There should be a period after the word "works," and the word "but" should start a new sentence.
   C. The words "filing" and "refiling" should be spelled "fileing" and "refileing."
   D. There should be a comma after the word "but."

8. The appeal was not considered because of its late arrival. 8.____
   A. This is an example of acceptable writing.
   B. The word "its" should be changed to "it's."
   C. The word "its" should be changed to "the."
   D. The words "late arrival" should be changed to "arrival late."

9. The letter must be read carefuly to determine under which subject it should be filed. 9.____
   A. This is an example of acceptable writing.
   B. The word "under" should be changed to "at."
   C. The word "determine" should be spelled "determin."
   D. The word "carefuly" should be spelled "carefully."

10. He showed potential as an office manager, but he lacked skill in delegating work. 10.____
   A. This is an example of acceptable writing.
   B. The word "delegating" should be spelled "delagating."
   C. The word "potential" should be spelled "potencial."
   D. The words "he lacked" should be changed to "was lacking."

KEY (CORRECT ANSWERS)

1.	D	6.	B
2.	B	7.	A
3.	C	8.	A
4.	D	9.	D
5.	A	10.	A

TEST 2

DIRECTIONS: Each question consists of a sentence which may or may not be an example of good English usage. Examine each sentence, considering grammar, punctuation, spelling, capitalization, and awkwardness. Then choose the correct statement about it from the four choices below it. If the English usage in the sentence given is better than any of the changes suggested in choices B, C, or D, pick choice A. (Do not pick a choice that will change the meaning of the sentence.) *PRINT THE LETTER OF THE CORRECT ANSWER IN THE SPACE AT THE RIGHT.*

1. The supervisor wants that all staff members report to the office at 9:00 A.M. 1.____
   A. This is an example of acceptable writing.
   B. The word "that" should be removed and the word "to" should be inserted after the word "members."
   C. There should be a comma after the word "wants" and a comma after the word "office."
   D. The word "wants" should be changed to "want" and the word "shall" should be inserted after the word "members."

2. Every morning the clerk opens the office mail and distributes it. 2.____
   A. This is an example of acceptable writing.
   B. The word "opens" should be changed to "open."
   C. The word "mail" should be changed to "letters."
   D. The word "it" should be changed to "them."

3. The secretary typed more fast on a desktop computer than on a laptop computer. 3.____
   A. This is an example of acceptable writing.
   B. The words "more fast" should be changed to "faster."
   C. There should be a comma after the words "desktop computer."
   D. The word "than" should be changed to "then."

4. The new stenographer needed a desk a computer, a chair and a blotter. 4.____
   A. This is an example of acceptable writing.
   B. The word "blotter" should be spelled "blodder."
   C. The word "stenographer" should begin with a capital letter.
   D. There should be a comma after the word "desk."

5. The recruiting officer said, "There are many different goverment jobs available." 5.____
   A. This is an example of acceptable writing.
   B. The word "There" should not be capitalized.
   C. The word "government" should be spelled "government."
   D. The comma after the word "said" should be removed.

6. He can recommend a mechanic whose work is reliable. 6.____
   A. This is an example of acceptable writing.
   B. The word "reliable" should be spelled "relyable."
   C. The word "whose" should be spelled "who's."
   D. The word "mechanic should be spelled "mecanic."

7. She typed quickly; like someone who had not a moment to lose. 7.____
   A. This is an example of acceptable writing.
   B. The word "not" should be removed.
   C. The semicolon should be changed to a comma.
   D. The word "quickly" should be placed before instead of after the word "typed."

8. She insisted that she had to much work to do. 8.____
   A. This is an example of acceptable writing.
   B. The word "insisted" should be spelled "incisted."
   C. The word "to" used in front of "much" should be spelled "too."
   D. The word "do" should be changed to "be done."

9. He excepted praise from his supervisor for a job well done. 9.____
   A. This is an example of acceptable writing.
   B. The word "excepted" should be spelled "accepted."
   C. The order of the words "well done" should be changed to "done well."
   D. There should be a comma after the word "supervisor."

10. What appears to be intentional errors in grammar occur several times in the passage. 10.____
   A. This is an example of acceptable writing.
   B. The word "occur" should be spelled "occurr."
   C. The word "appears" should be changed to "appear."
   D. The phrase "several times" should be changed to "from time to time."

KEY (CORRECT ANSWERS)

1.	B	6.	A
2.	A	7.	C
3.	B	8.	C
4.	D	9.	B
5.	C	10.	C

TEST 3

DIRECTIONS: Each question consists of a sentence which may or may not be an example of good English usage. Examine each sentence, considering grammar, punctuation, spelling, capitalization, and awkwardness. Then choose the correct statement about it from the four choices below it. If the English usage in the sentence given is better than any of the changes suggested in choices B, C, or D, pick choice A. (Do not pick a choice that will change the meaning of the sentence.) *PRINT THE LETTER OF THE CORRECT ANSWER IN THE SPACE AT THE RIGHT.*

1. The clerk could have completed the assignment on time if he knows where these materials were located. 1.____
   A. This is an example of acceptable writing.
   B. The word "knows" should be replaced by "had known."
   C. The word "were" should be replaced by "had been."
   D. The words "where these materials were located" should be replaced by "the location of these materials."

2. All employees should be given safety training. Not just those who accidents. 2.____
   A. This is an example of acceptable writing.
   B. The period after the word "training" should be changed to a colon.
   C. The period after the word "training" should be changed to a semicolon, and the first letter of the word "Not" should be changed to a small "n."
   D. The period after the word "training" should be changed to a comma, and the first letter of the word "Not" should be changed to a small "n."

3. This proposal is designed to promote employee awareness of the suggestion program, to encourage employee participation in the program, and to increase the number of suggestions submitted. 3.____
   A. This is an example of acceptable writing.
   B. The word "proposal" should be spelled "proposal."
   C. The words "to increase the number of suggestions submitted" should be changed to "an increase in the number of suggestions is expected."
   D. The word "promote" should be changed to "enhance" and the word "increase" should be changed to "add to."

4. The introduction of inovative managerial techniques should be preceded by careful analysis of the specific circumstances and conditions in each department. 4.____
   A. This is an example of acceptable writing.
   B. The word "technique" should be spelled "techneques."
   C. The word "inovative" should be spelled "innovative."
   D. A comma should be placed after the word "circumstances" and after the word "conditions."

5. This occurrence indicates that such criticism embarrasses him. 5.____
   A. This is an example of acceptable writing.
   B. The word "occurrence" should be spelled "occurence."
   C. The word "criticism" should be spelled "critisism.
   D. The word "embarrasses" should be spelled "embarasses.

KEY (CORRECT ANSWERS)

1. B
2. D
3. A
4. C
5. A

PREPARING WRITTEN MATERIAL

EXAMINATION SECTION

TEST 1

DIRECTIONS: Each short paragraph below is followed by four restatements or summaries of the information contained within it. Select the one that most completely and accurately states the information or opinion given in the paragraph. *PRINT THE LETTER OF THE CORRECT ANSWER IN THE SPACE AT THE RIGHT.*

1. Australia's koalas live solely on a diet of the leaves of the eucalyptus tree, a low-protein food that requires a koala to eat about three or four pounds of leaves a day. For most mammals, these strong-smelling leaves, saturated with toxins such as phenols and the oily compound known as cineole, are among the least digestible foods on the planet. However, the koala is equipped with a digestive system that is able to handle these toxins, trapping the tiniest leaf particles for as much as eight days while the sugars, proteins, and fats are extracted. 1.____

   A. Because eucalyptus leaves contain a large amount of toxins and oils, it takes a long time for koalas to digest them.
   B. Koalas have to eat three or four pounds of eucalyptus leaves a day, because the leaves are so poor in nutrients.
   C. Koalas have a unique digestive system that allows them to exist solely on a diet of eucalyptus leaves, which are generally toxic and inedible.
   D. The digestive system of the koala illustrates the unique evolutionary palette of the Australian continent.

2. Norway's special geopolitical position—it was the only NATO country to share a border with Russia—drove it to adopt much more cautious policies than other European countries during the Cold War. Its decision to join NATO led to strong protests from Russia, and in order to avoid provocation, Norway's foreign policy had to balance the need for ensuring defense capability with the need to keep tensions at the lowest possible level. Norway's low-tension "base policy" made clear the nation's refusal to allow foreign military forces on Norwegian territory as long as the country is not attacked or threatened with an attack. 2.____

   A. Norway's "base policy," in spite of its shared border with Russia, is the work of a pacifist nation that should serve as a model for foreign diplomacy everywhere.
   B. When Norway joined NATO, Russia feared a ground invasion over their shared border.
   C. The "base policy" of Norway is a perfect illustration on how much of Europe during the Cold War was a powder keg ready to explode at the slightest provocation.
   D. As the only member of the NATO alliance to border on Russia, Norway was forced to adopt a more conciliatory foreign policy than other members of the alliance.

3. During the women's suffrage movement of the early twentieth century, it was typical of many psychologists and anti-suffragists to automatically associate feminism with mental illness. In 1918, H.W. Frink wrote of feminists: "A certain proportion of at least the most militant suffragists are neurotics who in some instances are compensating for masculine trends, in others, are more or less successfully sublimating sadistic and homosexual ones." In the United States, anti-suffragists, finding comfort in psychology, concluded that suffragists all bordered hysteria and, thus, their arguments could not be taken seriously, 3.____
   A. The relationship between suffragism and feminism led many scientists to conclude that suffragists were afflicted with some kinds of mental illness.
   B. During the women's suffrage movement, anti-suffragists such as H.W. Frink tended to label women who fought for voting rights as mentally ill in order to dismiss their arguments.
   C. Responses to the women's suffrage movement are indicative of the tendency to label those who challenge the status quo as "Crazy" than to comfort their arguments.
   D. Most of the women who fought for suffrage during the early twentieth century were feminists who were mentally ill.

4. All of the earth's early plant life lived in the ocean, and most of these plants were concentrated in the shallow coastal waters, where the sun's energy could be easily absorbed. Because of the constant advance and retreat of tides in these regions, the plants—mostly algae—were repeatedly exposed to the atmosphere, and were forced to adapt to life out of water. It took millions of years before plant species had evolved that could survive out of the sea altogether, with stems that drew water from the ground, and a waxy covering to keep them from drying in the sun. 4.____
   A. After spending millions of years underwater, the earth's plants finally evolved ways of surviving on land.
   B. Most algaes today, because of evolutionary advances, are able to survive for extended periods of time out of water.
   C. Despite the fact that plants began as purely underwater organisms, they have always needed the sun's energy to survive.
   D. Land plants evolved from sea plants after millions of years in response to the gradual warming of the earth's atmosphere.

5. Because of the unique convergence of mild temperature and abundant rain (17 feet a year), British Columbia's temperate coastal rainforest is the most biologically productive ecosystem on earth. It's also an increasingly rare and vulnerable ecosystem: in its Holocene heyday, it covered only 0.2 percent of the earth's land surface. Today, logging and other development have consumed more than half this original range. 5.____
   A. The uniquely productive ecosystem of British Columbia's coastal rainforest has always been small, and has been reduced by human activity.
   B. Despite the fact that it is the most biologically productive ecosystem on earth, the coastal rainforest of British Columbia has been largely ignored by environmental activists.

C. The coastal rainforests of British Columbia have been nearly devastated by logging and other development.
D. British Columbia's coastal rainforest originated during the Holocene Era, but has declined steadily ever since.

6. The Roman Empire, which ruled much of the Western world for hundreds of years, was led by an aristocratic class famous for its tendency to drink large amounts of wine. Recently, an American medical researcher theorized that this taste for wine was eventually what caused the decline and fall of the empire—not the drinking of the wine itself, but a gradual poisoning from the lead that was used to line and seal Roman wine casks. The researcher, Dr. S.C. Gilfillan, argues that this lead poisoning specifically affected members of the Empire's ruling class, because they were the Romans most likely to consume wine and other products, like preserved fruits, that were stored in lead-lined jars. 6.____
A. The Roman aristocracy's taste for wine and dried fruits, according to one researcher, is a cautionary tale about the consequences of overindulgence.
B. While the Roman Empire's ruling class suffered from widespread lead poisoning, most commoners remained in good health throughout the empire.
C. One of the most far-fetched theories about the fall of the Roman Empire concerns itself with the lead used to line the wine casks and fruit jars of the ruling class.
D. An American medical researcher has theorized that the fall of the Roman Empire was caused by slow poisoning from the lead used to line and seal Roman wine casks and fruit jars.

7. In the second century B.C., King Hiero of Syracuse called upon the renowned scientist, Archimedes, to find a way to see if his crown was made of pure gold or a combination of metals. Archimedes came upon the solution some time later, as he was entering a tub full of hot water and noticed that the weight of his body displaced a certain amount of water. Realizing that this same principle could be used on the crown, he forgot himself with excitement, jumping out of the tub and running naked through the town, yellow "Eureka! Eureka!" 7.____
A. Archimedes, in making his famous discovery, unknowingly contributed the word "Eureka!" to the English vocabulary.
B. The relative purity of gold can be determined by the amount of water it displaces when submerged.
C. Archimedes, after discovering the solution to a scientific problem while stepping into his tub, became so excited that he ran through the town naked.
D. The word "Eureka" has become a part of the English language because of an interesting story involving the ancient scientist, Archimedes.

8. In the nineteenth century most Americans had never heard of, let alone tasted, an abalone, the marine mollusk considered to be a delicacy by many Asians, and undisturbed abalone populations thrived all along the west coast. When the California Gold Rush of the 1840s and 1850s brought thousands of Asian 8.____

immigrants to America, many of these people began to harvest the dense beds of abalone that inhabited the state's intertidal zone. The Asian harvests eventually brought in annual catches of over 4 million pounds of abalone, and as a result, some county governments passed ordinances making it illegal to dive for abalone in waters less than twenty feet deep.

A. The Asians who immigrated to California during the Gold Rush harvested so much abalone from intertidal waters that some governments were compelled to limit abalone diving.
B. Abalone diving was unheard of in California before the Gold Rush, when many Asians immigrated to the state and began to harvest abalone from the intertidal zone.
C. The extreme shortage of abalone in California's intertidal waters can be traced to the Asians who immigrated during the Gold Rush.
D. The abalone of California's coastal waters generally live in waters less than twenty feet deep, where they are not protected by most county governments.

9. Maria Tallchief, the daughter of a full-blood Osage Indian from Oklahoma, was America's first internationally celebrated prima ballerina, rising to stardom at a time when classical American ballet was still struggling to gain international acceptance and acclaim. Her innovative interpretations of such classics as "Swan Lake" and "The Nutcracker" helped convince critics worldwide that American ballet was a force to be reckoned with, and her glamorous beauty helped popularize ballet in America at a time when very few people took it seriously. 9.____

A. As ballet grew more popular in America, Maria Tallchief became a phenomenon in Europe, helping to secure a worldwide reputation for excellence for American ballet.
B. Nobody in America took ballet seriously until the beautiful Maria Tallchief became an international star.
C. With her beauty and technical innovations, Maria Tallchief gained unprecedented critical and popular success for American ballet.
D. Before the success of Maria Tallchief, there were not many ballet dancers in the United States worth noticing.

10. Early in the Constitutional Convention of 1787, the idea of a two-tiered legislature was agreed upon by the framers of the Constitution. The final form of each of the resulting houses, however, was an issue that was debated openly, and which was finally resolved by the "great compromise" of the Constitutional Convention. While the House of Representatives was intended to be a large, politically sensitive body, the Senate was designed to be a moderating influence that would check the powers of the House. 10.____

A. The framers of the Constitution could not agree on whether the nation's legislature should be bicameral, or two-tiered, at first, but after the "great compromise," they devised a House and Senate.
B. The Constitutional Convention of 1787 ended with the "great compromise" that gave the nation its two-tiered legislature.

C. After much behind-the-scenes dealmaking, the two-tiered legislature of the United States was devised by the framers of the Constitution.
D. The framers of the Constitution, after some debate, decided on a two-tiered legislature made up of a House of Representatives and a Senate that was less susceptible to regional politics.

11. Although scientists have succeeded in creating robots able to process huge amounts of information, they are still struggling to create one whose reasoning ability matches that of a human baby. The main challenge facing these scientists is the difficulty of understanding and imitating the complex process of human perception and reasoning, which involve the ability to register and analyze even the smallest changes in the external environment, and then to act on those changes. 11.____
A. Even the most sophisticated robot is unable to imitate innate human abilities such as learning to walk, converse, or perceive depth.
B. Because of their inability to process large amounts of information, robots have yet to achieve even the most fundamental level of reasoning.
C. Despite considerable technological advances, scientists have as yet been unable to produce a robot that can respond intelligently to changes in its environment.
D. Because robots cannot automatically filter out all extraneous information and focus on the most important details of a given situation, they are unable to reason as well as humans.

12. Thor Heyerdahl, a Norwegian anthropologist, had long held the opinion that the Polynesian inhabitants of South Pacific islands such as Samoa, Tonga, and Fiji had actually been migrants from South America. To prove that this was possible, in1947 Heyerdahl made a crude raft out of balsa wood, which he named after an Incan sun god, *Kon-Tiki*, and sailed from the coast of Peru to the islands east of Tahiti. 12.____
A. Thor Heyerdahl's 1947 voyage on the *Kon-Tiki* proved that Polynesians probably had common ancestors in South America.
B. While Thor Heyerdahl's *Kon-Tiki* voyage suggested a South American origin for Polynesians, most experts today believe the great migrations were launched from somewhere near Indonesia.
C. To support the idea that Polynesians could have sailed from South America to the Pacific Islands, Thor Heyerdahl sailed the *Kon-Tiki* from Peru to Tahiti in 1947.
D. Thor Heyerdahl's famous raft, the *Kon-Tiki*, was named for an Incan sun god, and was so well-made that it made it from Peru to Tahiti.

13. During the Age of Exploration, after thousands of miles of open sea, ships entered the bays of the Azore Islands, west of Portugal, with tattered sails, battered hulls, crewmen weakened from scurvy, and cargo holds laden with the treasure they had gained on their long trading journeys. Spanish, English, and Dutch warships prowled the waters around the Azores to protect this treasure, sometimes even sinking their own ships to keep it from falling into enemy 13.____

hands. During these fierce battles, many ships filled with treasure were sent to the ocean floor, where they still remain, preserved by the cold saltwater and centuries of rest.

A. Although they are now sparsely populated, the Azore Islands were once a resting place for every ship returning from a long journey to the Americas.
B. Many treasure hunters and archaeologists believe the sea floor around the Azores, a group of islands west of Portugal, still harbors some of the richest sunken treasure in the world.
C. Economic competition between the European powers was so intense during the Age of Exploration that captains would rather sink their own ships rather than let their treasure fall into enemy hands.
D. The rich history of the Azore Islands has deposited a large amount of sunken treasure in their surrounding waters.

14. The Whigs, a short-lived American political party, were wary of a domineering president, and many of them believed that the legislative branch should govern the nation. In particular, Whig leader Henry Clay often attempted to bully and belittle President John Tyler into submission. Tyler's resistance to Clay's high-handed tactics strengthened the office of the presidency, and in particular gave greater credibility to all later vice presidents who happened to succeed to the office. 14.____

A. While U.S. politics was at first dominated by the legislature, President John Tyler shifted the center of power to the presidency, while laying the groundwork for the downfall of the Whig Party.
B. President John Tyler, a failure by almost any other measure, can at least be credited with contributing to the strength of the presidency.
C. Henry Clay, who believed in a strong legislature, failed to win much influence over presidents who were not from the Whig Party.
D. President John Tyler, in resisting Henry Clay's bullying tactics, strengthened the U.S. presidency and lent credibility to the authority of vice presidential successors to the presidency.

15. By far the richest city on earth, Tokyo, Japan is also one of the most over-crowded; most of its people are only able to afford living in extremely small houses and apartments. In addition to cramped housing, Tokyo's overpopulation has created a commuter problem so grim that a corps of "pushers" has been hired by the city, to stand outside crowded commuter trains and help pack people inside. Problems such as these are so severe in Tokyo that there has been serious talk in recent years of moving Japan's capital elsewhere. 15.____

A. Despite the example of Tokyo, there is no evidence to suggest that economic wealth and overpopulation are related variables.
B. Tokyo's prosperity has led to such overcrowding that the country of Japan has recently begun to consider moving its capital to another location.
C. Despite being the richest city on earth, Tokyo, Japan is seriously overcrowded.
D. The small houses and apartments in Tokyo, along with its overcrowded transit system, are a perfect example of how economic wealth does not always improve a society's quality of life.

16. One of the greatest, and least publicized, legacies of Native American culture has been the worldwide cultivation of food staples through careful farming methods. Over centuries, tribes throughout North and South America domesticated the wild plants that have come to produce over half of the vegetables the world eats today. Corn, or maize, was first cultivated in the Mexican highlands almost seven thousand years ago, from a common wild grass called teosinte, and both potatoes and tomatoes were originally domesticated by the Peruvian Incas from native plants that still grow throughout Peru and Bolivia. 16.____
   A. Explorers of the Americas carried many native vegetables back to Europe, where they continued to adapt and flourish over the centuries.
   B. Today's common corn is a descendent of the wild Mexican teosinte plant, and potatoes and tomatoes were originally grown by the Incas.
   C. Without the agricultural knowledge and skill of early Native Americans, much of the world today would be in danger of famine.
   D. Foods that are today grown and eaten almost worldwide, such as corn, tomatoes, and potatoes, were first cultivated by the natives of North and South Americas.

17. America's transportation sector—95 percent of it driven by oil—consumes two-thirds of the petroleum used in the United States. With the 400 million cars now on the world's roads expected to grow to 1 billion by the year 2020, oil-foreign or not and other finite fossil-fuel resources will some day be conversation pieces for the nostalgic, rather than components of the nation's energy mix. 17.____
   A. In the future, most motor vehicles in the United States will be powered by an alternative energy source such as hydrogen or solar power.
   B. The continued growth of the oil-dependent transportation sector is outpacing the capacity of fossil-fuel energy resources.
   C. Our nation's dependence on foreign oil is a serious vulnerability that can only be corrected by increased domestic production.
   D. In the future, 1 billion cars across the world will be competing for oil and gasoline.

18. Althea Gibson, the first African-American to win the Wimbledon Tennis Championship, began her career by riding the subway out of her neighborhood in Harlem to 143rd Street, where she played paddle tennis against anyone who dared to challenge her. Since the Wimbledon tournament was played on grass, Gibson knew she would have to prepare herself by training on a surface that returned balls as quickly as a grass court. She found the solution to this problem in the gyms of Harlem, whose wood floors allowed her to perfect the rapid volley that helped her win two Wimbledon championships. 18.____
   A. Althea Gibson's tennis skills, including her famous volley, were developed in and around the inner-city neighborhood of Harlem.
   B. Althea Gibson had to leave her neighborhood to learn tennis, but to perfect her game, she had to return home to Harlem.
   C. Without the wood floors in the gyms of her Harlem neighborhood, Althea Gibson probably wouldn't have developed a volley that would help her win two Wimbledon tennis championships.

D. Although Althea Gibson achieved international fame as the first African-American to win the Wimbledon Tennis Championship, the path she followed to that championship was as unorthodox as the champion herself.

19. The greenhouse effect is a naturally occurring process that aids in heating the Earth's surface and atmosphere. It results from the fact that certain atmospheric gases, such as carbon dioxide, water vapor, and methane, are able to change the energy balance of the planet by being able to absorb longwave radiation from the Earth's surface. Without the greenhouse effect, life on this planet would probably not exist, as the average temperature of the Earth would be a chilly 5 degrees, rather than the present 59 degrees. 19.____

A. The naturally-occurring greenhouse effect, by which atmospheric air is warmed, enables life to exist on earth.
B. The greenhouse effect is a completely natural phenomenon that has nothing to do with human activity, and in fact it is beneficial to the planet's ecosystems.
C. Human contributions to the increases in the greenhouse effect threaten life on Earth.
D. In order for life to exist on Earth there must be some kind of greenhouse effect.

20. The religious and scientific communities have for centuries been at odds with each other, and held opposing viewpoints concerning the origin and nature of life. Progressive thinkers from both groups, however, claim that the two communities, in their ways of seeking answers to humanity's most important questions, share a common set of goals and procedures that would benefit greatly from a cooperative effort. 20.____

A. Scientists and theologists will probably never agree on the origin and nature of life, though some progressive thinkers are trying to change the way the two communities talk about these issues.
B. Though most scientists do not believe in God, progressive religious thinkers are continually trying to persuade them otherwise.
C. Progressive religious and scientific thinkers have identified shared goals and questions that the two communities can work together to achieve and solve.
D. Religious thinkers, who usually scorn such scientific theories as evolution, have begun to acknowledge the usefulness of science in answering important questions.

21. The administrations of Presidents Richard Nixon and Jimmy Carter oversaw an Export-Import Bank that was increasingly active in trade promotion, with expanding programs and lending authority. During this period, expenditures for program activities expanded to five times their 1969 rate, but the bank's net income dropped sharply—the low interest rates at which the bank financed its loan programs were lowering its profits. 21.____

A. During the Nixon and Carter administrations, the budget of the Export-Import Bank grew to five times its 1969 expenditures.

B. Though the Export-Import Bank was very active during the Nixon and Carter administrations, its profits were reduced by its low interest rates.
C. Both the Nixon and Carter administrations demonstrated a lack of fiscal discipline that led to a declining net income at the Export-Import Bank.
D. Presidents Nixon and Carter both favored an activist Export-Import Bank, but while Nixon emphasized the function of trade promotion, Carter was more focused on making loans.

22. The Kombai and Korawai tribes of eastern Indonesia are known as the "tree people" for their custom of living in large tree houses, built as high as 150 feet above ground to avoid attacks from their enemies. These houses are built mostly from the fronds of the sago palm, a plant that also serves to produce one of the tree people's primary food sources—the larvae, or grub, of the scarab beetle. The tree people cultivate grubs by cutting a stretch of sago forest and then, after splitting and tying the palms together, leaving the palms to rot. 22.____

A. The food-gathering methods of the Kombai and Korawai illustrate that deforestation is not a contemporary problem.
B. The Kombai and Korawai people of eastern Indonesia relay on the sago palm for both food and housing.
C. The Kombai and Korawai fears of enemy attacks have led them to build their trees high in the forest canopy
D. Among the world's least-tamed native cultures are the Kombai and Korawai of Irian Jaya, the easternmost region of Indonesia.

23. It's no secret that corporate and federal information networks continue to deal with increasing bandwidth needs. The appetite for data—whether it's for internet access, file delivery, or the integration of digital voice applications—isn't likely to level off any time soon, and most information technology professionals allow that there is cause for concern. But emerging technologies for increasing raw bandwidth, accompanied by the streaming and maturing of transfer and switching protocols, are a good bet to accommodate the hunger for bandwidth, at least into the near future. 23.____

A. There are two ways to decrease the demand for more bandwidth over computer networks: either increase the "raw" amount of bandwidth over an infrastructure, or devise more efficient transfer and switching protocols.
B. Emerging technologies, aimed at the constantly increasing demand for bandwidth, are some day likely to result in virtually unlimited bandwidth for computer networks.
C. Many different applications contribute to the demand for bandwidth over a computer network, and so the technologies that are devised to meet this demand must be many-faceted.
D. While there is always a need for more bandwidth on large computer networks, newer technologies promise to increase the supply in the near term.

24. In the year 805, a Japanese Buddhist monk named Dengyo Daishi returned from his studies in China with some tea seeds, which he planted on a Japanese mountainside. In China, tea had long been the favorite drink of monks, because it helped them stay awake and attentive during their long periods of meditation, and Dengyo Daishi wanted to bring this practice to Japan. Over the centuries, tea-drinking would prove to be a custom that would influence nearly every aspect of Japanese culture, and Dengyo Daishi has long been considered a sort of saint among the Japanese. 24.____

A. Because of the cultural similarities between China and Japan, it was only a matter of time before the ritual of tea-drinking made its way from the mainland to the island empire.
B. Dengo Daishi, the first person to plant tea seeds in Japan, is revered among today's Japanese.
C. The Japanese tea-drinking custom was begun in 805 by a Buddhist monk who brought tea seeds from China.
D. Without the shared cultural traditions of Buddhism, it is unlikely that tea ever would have been imported from China to Japan.

25. Aztec women held a position in society that was far more respected than that of women in most Western civilizations of the time. For example, an Aztec wife was free to divorce a man who failed to provide for their children, or who was physically abusive, and once divorced, a woman was free to remarry whomever she chose. Perhaps the unusually high regard for Aztec women is best illustrated by the traditional Aztec religious belief that a special, elevated status in the afterlife was reserved for only two types of Aztec citizens-warriors who had died defending their tribe, and woman who had died during childbirth. 25.____

A. The rights and privileges of Aztec women demonstrate that they were more respected by their societies than women of many cultures of the time.
B. In the Aztec culture, women had the same rights and status as the most exalted men.
C. Though the rights of Aztec women were still generally inferior to those of men, most Aztec women were granted a high degree of independence due to their service to the community.
D. The relatively high position that Aztec women held in their society reveals the Aztec culture to be well ahead of its time.

KEY (CORRECT ANSWERS)

1.	C	11.	C
2.	D	12.	C
3.	B	13.	D
4.	A	14.	D
5.	A	15.	B
6.	D	16.	D
7.	C	17.	B
8.	A	18.	A
9.	C	19.	A
10.	D	20.	C

21.	B
22.	B
23.	D
24.	C
25.	A

www.ingramcontent.com/pod-product-compliance
Lightning Source LLC
Chambersburg PA
CBHW082210300426
44117CB00016B/2740